Praise For I³ for

"No marriage can become (or remain) healthy and strong without consistent attention. In his new book, I3 for Couples, Dr. Stewart applies the concepts of emotional intelligence to the context of marriage. In doing so, he provides the reader with a wealth of practical tools that can be used to help your marriage stand the test of time. I have known Greg both personally and professionally for over 20 years, and the lessons shared in this book have been hard-earned. Do yourself a favor...read this book, do what it says, and experience the fullness of what marriage was intended to be."

Brian Clark, MBA

This book is filled with many valuable insights, but the one that resonated with me the most was this powerful statement: "Grace and empathy without truth and boundaries is enablement, and truth and boundaries without grace and empathy is toxic." It's a profound reminder of the balance we all need in setting healthy boundaries. For anyone who struggles with defining their boundaries, navigating relationships, and understanding their emotions, this book is both timely and impactful.

Shelly Gloyna, LPC, EMDR Certified

Marriage is not for the faint-of-heart, but a marriage that experiences emotional safety and connection is worth more than gold. Dr. Stewart, based on his training, study, and decades of experience in working with couples, has been able to pull together a rich addition to the writings on marriage that is poised to boost any couple's longed-for marital content experience.

Ingo Tophoven, PhD, LPC
Assistant Professor of Counseling
Gordon Conwell Theological Seminary - Charlotte

I dedicate this book to every marriage. I believe that every person wants to experience an incredibly powerful marriage. Not only that, but every person also wants to give their spouse an incredibly powerful marriage. My hope is this book will help every person achieve those goals.

I am my beloved's and my beloved is mine . . .

- *Song of Songs 6:3*

Table of Contents

Acknowledgements i

Foreword 1

Introduction 4

Chapter 1: The Emotional Goals of Marriage 7

Chapter 2: Blind to What You Cannot See 27

Chapter 3: Our Emotional Storms 48

Chapter 4: The Matrix of Insecurity 61

Chapter 5: Leave the Window Open for Tinkerbell 68

Chapter 6: Stop Causing Further Damage 84

Chapter 7: Scheduling the Minimum 118

Chapter 8: I Have Never Been Loved Like This Before 132

Chapter 9: I^3 – Information, Interpretation, Intensity 146

Appendix A: Recovering from Failures 158

Appendix B: Parenting 172

Foreword

What do you do when your car battery lacks the electrical energy to start your car? The obvious answer is that you connect your red (positive) and black (negative) terminals to another car. The electrical current produced by the operating motor is transferred through copper cables to empower your car. We call it "a jump"

For couples whose battery is low, this book is voltage. If you need a "jump", read this book. Dr. Greg Stewart confronts the tendency for couples to stare at their engine, scratch their respective scalps and hopelessly declare, "Yep, this car battery is dead", then stare at other cars as they drive by at freeway speeds, or couples may cast blame, "I knew the battery was weak. I told you that we should have gotten this fixed weeks ago. Now we are stuck here in the middle of nowhere!"

Dr. Stewart honors the painful and frustrating lament, the emotion experienced when marriages, like our vehicles, do not work as they are intended and recognizes the severe danger. Our emotional reactivity—our mad, sad or afraid reactions can prompt us to feel awful yet do nothing—except blame one another and not change. He writes, "He or she may trigger you, but the amount of your negative emotions and the solution to your negative emotions rests entirely with you, not them."

This book is an instruction manual for couples—perhaps better stated, it is for individuals who are coupled. The focus is how to redirect energy, to jump start the car battery and get back on the road. His instruction is practical, direct and measurable. He draws from the deep well of Biblical wisdom. It is not a "3-steps to an easy life", but a disciplined, determined directive to become gracious, loving and kind.

Dr. Stewart uses a simple four-word acronym to prompt us to assess, alter and achieve necessary changes--RHWR. He suggests that we ask ourselves and our beloved if the solutions implemented to better our lives are Rational, Healthy, Wise, and Right. If they are not, then we work together in moving towards solutions.

I find an essential declaration essential for every person in relationship to declare. It is, "This is my "problem, concern, pattern or reaction". I take full responsibility for it." When two people in relationship identify in themselves the contribution they make for the stalled marriage, they are on the path to recovery. The successful declaration of that statement can lead to a request which causes car engines to roar and marriages to accelerate. After declaring the responsibility for a problem comes the question, "Will you help me?" That is why we have marriage. Life is hard and we need help.

My suggestion, read this book. Follow his methods—red is positive, black is negative. Jump start the engine and get down the road.

James Sells, Ph.D.

Hughes Endowed Chair of Christian Thought in Mental Health Practice

Professor, School of Psychology & Counseling, Counseling Department, Regent University

Preface

I wrote this book because I have worked with hundreds upon hundreds of couples, and I believe the system I created for helping marriages is extremely effective. I go beyond the normal discussion of emotions and desires to give couples effective action steps and techniques to improve their marriage, as well as measurable ways to objectively assess ourselves as spouses. I also wrote this book because I have been divorced, and what I discovered about myself since that time has been invaluable in strengthening my heart. My previous book, *I³ Unlock the Inner Strength Behind Your Negative Emotions* explained my journey-turned-counseling theory process for how I faced my own issues that led to the failure of my first marriage. Further, my second marriage is phenomenal, and my wife and I often say that we don't know how our marriage can get any better. We are safe with one another, and we pursue one another hard. It's amazing! We want you to experience what we experience, and I pray this book helps you do that.

Introduction

You are all fair, my love, and there is no spot in you. – Song of Songs 4:7

This book is a supplement to my first book, *I³ Information, Interpretation, Intensity: Unlock the Inner Strength Behind Your Negative Emotions*. The idea of this book was actually a bit of an accident. When I was writing I³ (pronounced "I cubed"), I started promoting my book on social media. Prior to beginning to write, the only social media I had was LinkedIn, and I had zero experience as an "influencer" (I think that's what they call it). Needless to say, I was far removed from the generations that grew up on it. I created a variety of videos and quotes discussing parts of my book. One day, I had the idea of doing short videos where I discussed marriage principles and techniques. I am currently a full-time therapist, and half my caseload is working with couples, therefore it was easy for me to come up with content. Without even thinking, I began the video by saying, "Welcome to I³ for couples!" Attempting to be strategic, I wanted to link everything back to my book. After several videos, I started to realize there was a great degree of overlap between the concepts from my book and the undercurrent of the relationship dynamics I saw with my married couples. It should have been more apparent to me that all the material I was writing to help individuals *unlock the inner strength behind their negative emotions* could be translated to couples. Afterall, a couple is made up of two individuals. Don't judge me. I have a PhD, but sometimes I can be really slow on the uptake.

I was already using the same material with couples, but it did not even cross my mind to write another book using the same title until I started creating the Instagram reels. Once the idea was born, it took off, and I began to conceptualize how I would write this book. I wanted to repeat many of the exact same principles, assuming that many of you did not read my first book. Book sales aside, I do strongly encourage you to read that book as well because both books have the key foundational premise that we need to remove the environment from all initial processing of our negative emotions, which includes our spouse. It would be prudent for you to isolate yourself and do a deep dive into your own heart and identity to gain full authority and management of your identity, value, and worth. I'll primarily frame this book in the context of marriage, but I want to make one thing clear: your emotional autonomy and independence are not tied to your relationship status. Success in this journey isn't about being in a relationship with a significant other, fiancé, or spouse; it's about developing your own emotional strength and resilience, regardless of your relationship status.

On the other side of the proverbial coin, the more successful you are in unlocking the strength behind your personal negative emotions, the more powerful and fulfilling your marriage will be. While I weave in most of the main principles from my first book into the context of marriage, the lion's share of this book will be about the vision for marriage, communication skills and techniques, and my system for helping couples be fully alive in their marriage. I pray this book achieves just that. However, the gateway to its success is the foundational assertion that *successful counseling (growth) begins and ends with the client. I don't have the power to change anyone.* At this stage in my career, I can confidently declare to every individual client and every couple that I promise to equip them with the skills to be successful. Be open, be teachable, and have the courage to overcome the fear of your deepest insecurities being exposed because it is there you will find your confidence, your power, your rest, and your peace.

CHAPTER 1:

THE EMOTIONAL GOALS OF MARRIAGE

You have ravished my heart... With one look of your eyes. - Song of Songs 4:9

Everything we do is an attempt to achieve an emotional goal.

Why date? Why get married? What emotional goal were you trying to achieve when you wanted to be the boyfriend or girlfriend of your first crush? What emotional goal were you trying to achieve when you "explained away" the reasons why that crush declined your invitation? Everything we do as humans, everything, is to achieve an emotional goal. When we are in pursuit of a particular emotional goal, we try to increase our quality of life. We do this by either doing something that produces positive emotions or doing something to avoid negative emotions. The problem we are trying to solve is actually the obstacle keeping us from experiencing positive emotions. We attempt to increase our positive emotions (emotional goal) by convincing our childhood crush to go steady with us. If that goal is blocked, it produces negative emotions. We then try and achieve the emotional goal of removing those negative emotions by attacking what we perceive to be the obstacle to our emotional goal. The obstacle could be that our childhood crush has their own crush (the jerky jock or the bubbleheaded blonde), so we attack their crush to diminish the value of that person in our crush's mind; or it could be we attack ourselves. *If I wasn't such a loser, my crush would fall for me.* Finally, for us hopeless romantics, the obstacle is that our crush simply isn't aware of how awesome we are, so we insist on selling ourselves to them to remove the obstacle of ignorance. Everything is about trying to achieve those emotional goals.

Breaking it down even further and expanding the context of our emotional goals, we all are, at any given moment, trying to achieve both micro and macro emotional goals. Micro emotional goals are immediate, here-and-now emotional goals. Our day-to-day behaviors illustrate how we achieve our micro emotional goals. We eat to *feel* full, drink to *not feel* thirsty, shower to *feel* clean, pet our dogs to *feel* their soft fur and *feel* love, go to the store to *feel* secure because we have food for our family, and watch a movie to *feel* a temporary escape from the stress of our lives. At the same time, we try to achieve our macro emotional goals, which is our overall quality of life, broken down into three categories: *increasing our standard of living* (dating our crush), *living our values, beliefs, and philosophy of life* (I date to eventually get married), and to feel peace by living a life of purpose and meaning by *fulfilling our destiny* (getting married, raising a family, and passing down our legacy). Every moment we live, our micro goals are ever present, while our macro goals are always in our peripheral vision. As we go about achieving our emotional goals, we feel negative emotions when those goals are blocked. Thus, we try many ways to solve the problem responsible for the negative emotions.

Emotional Goals vs. Rational, Healthy, Wise, and Right (RHWR) Paths

It is important to differentiate our emotional goals from the paths (behaviors, actions, choices) we take to achieve those emotional goals. Our emotional goals are good, healthy, and beautiful. The problem is in the paths we take to achieve those emotional goals. These paths could be rational or irrational, healthy or unhealthy, wise or unwise, right or wrong. We are often focused on feeling something different (micro and macro emotional goals), we impulsively just *do* without assessing if we're taking the right means to get to our end. Our goal is always good, but if we choose the wrong path, we run into a whole host of problems. Even though we know our paths are harmful, we make the mistake of connecting the path with the emotional goal, rather than seeing them as separate entities. When someone, like our partner, points out our non-RHWR path (that is to say a means of getting what we want that is not Rational, Healthy, Wise, and Right), we get defensive and angry (negative emotions) because we feel our partner is blocking our emotional goals, which is absolutely not true.

Mental Model Formula Formation: There are several paths we can choose to achieve our emotional goals.

I frequently hear people argue over their paths, staunchly defending their preferred path as if it were the only way. The truth is, there are several different paths to achieve any emotional goal. When we make this separation, it is much easier to agree with our partners, own our actions were not RHWR, and then choose a better RHWR path to achieve our emotional goal. When we stop to realize there are several paths to achieve our emotional goals, we can loosen our emotional grip on a particular path, especially if that path causes issues for us or others around us. We burn way too much emotional energy over paths! Take a moment and examine yourself to see how this applies. What behaviors, choices, and habits do you need to change? What emotional goals are you trying to achieve by these paths? What other RHWR paths are available to you to achieve the same emotional goals?

You probably have heard the phrase, "the end justifies the means." This phrase means that it is okay to do whatever it takes, even if it's wrong, to accomplish your goal. But we all know that the end doesn't justify the means. While the end goal may be good, the means to get there can still be bad or harmful. Thus remains the main idea of this chapter: separate the goal (end) from the path (means), and the need to evaluate the path (means) we use to accomplish our end (emotional goals). I'm assuming we all agree with this and are aware we should change some of our paths (means), such as our choices, actions, behaviors, responses, and habits. Yet, the question remains, "Why is it so difficult to change once and for all and relinquish the paths causing us pain and harming our relationships? Why do we return to them?" As you and I sit here today, do a quick scan of your paths and life circumstances. Identify a few areas where you would like your life improved. Sort these changes into two columns: *changes in ourselves* and *changes in our environment*. What is your strategy to make these changes in each of these columns? What is your strategy for changing yourself? What is your strategy for changing your environment? If you believe you have a good strategy, but your success rate of change in each column is low, then what stories are you telling yourself to explain why it's not working?

As humans, we are more committed to what's familiar than what is healthy. Even though it may be dysfunctional, we are more comfortable with what we are used to (our habits), and it takes a lot of work to change those habits. Furthermore, we are all very committed to emotional self-preservation from negative emotions, such as the feeling we are failing overall or are a "loser" because we can't change. These feelings are part of being human. Even if we have already committed to making certain changes but are unsuccessful, we get frustrated and discouraged. Helping you become successful is the subject of an innumerable number of books, and many have great techniques. I hope to add to a list of techniques to assist you. My focus is trying to help you better understand the role negative emotions play in the process. They don't "feel" good, but that's the point! Sure, there is a way to get rid of them – by changing! When we don't change when we know we should, we get defensive and commit what is called the *fundamental attribution error*. The Fundamental Attribution error is a psychological term that states we attribute other's failures and shortcomings to who they are as a person. In other words, their character is flawed. But when explaining the reason for our lack of success, we blame our environment and circumstances. Very rarely do we blame ourselves. Be honest, how many times have you been angry with your partner and judged their maturity, character, and motives when they did something that was not RHWR?

Conversely, when you did something that wasn't RHWR, you defended yourself by describing the difficult situation you were in, the stress you were under, or the pain you were experiencing. We all commit this double standard of judgment. We all experience difficult circumstances, but if there was another path that was RHWR we could have taken, then we need to own it by admitting that regardless of the situation we were in, we should not have selected the non-RHWR path we did.

We choose our paths for a variety of reasons, so let's begin the process of how to evaluate why we choose a given path. The easiest paths to evaluate involve behaviors we already know we want to change. What is it about that path that makes it bad? Is the path irrational? When you commit the fundamental attribution error, you are being irrational by attributing your weaknesses to your circumstances at the time and blaming other's weaknesses on their flawed character. Is your path unhealthy? Raising your voice at others and name-calling is not healthy. Is your path unwise? You really want your children to have a great Christmas, but you go into debt to achieve that goal. Is your path wrong? You hold others to a standard of behavior that you don't live up to, and you make excuses for yourself, again resorting to the fundamental attribution error. Take a moment to check in. Are you experiencing negative emotions because of what I'm suggesting?

While doing this, practice simultaneously identifying the emotional goal you are trying to achieve. In each unwanted behavior (path), ask yourself, "When I do that behavior (choose this path), what am I trying to feel?" Be as specific as possible; find the perfect word, such as *significant, successful, respected*. Then, assess why the path you chose is not Rational, Healthy, Wise, or Right (what I call the RHWR grid). Own it and even apologize for it if you need to. Next, brainstorm and come up with as many RHWR paths as you can that would accomplish that same emotional goal in the future. The process helps equip your brain with alternatives in the future, so it doesn't default to habitual non-RHWR behavior. This works well for the micro process (immediate, here-and-now emotional goals). Now, let's discuss the macro process (overall quality of life).

What do you yearn to be different about your life? Your standard of living? Your accomplishments? Your career? When you answer these questions, you are choosing paths. Some of you might have answered the first question by wanting to feel different (less anxiety), which is fine, but is a micro goal, let's stick to tangible quality-of-life changes (macro goals). Once you define these paths, describe the emotional goal you are trying to achieve via that path. For example, earning a bachelor's degree is not the goal; it is the path we choose to take to achieve the emotional goal of feeling more accomplished, or it may be part of a goal to get a job that pays significantly more, to achieve the emotional goal of an increased standard of living. When we understand it in this way, we realize that there are several paths we can take to achieve our true goal, which is always emotional in nature. There are several paths for me to choose to feel more successful; getting a bachelor's degree is just one path. I could get certifications, work on getting promoted, or getting a raise, or learning a new skill to feel more successful.

Now, let's explore our deeper emotional goals of feeling accepted, feeling like we belong, feeling secure, feeling successful and significant, and feeling value and worth in our identity. What paths are you taking to achieve these emotional goals? What are your paths of response when someone blocks your path to achieve one of these goals? When someone corrects us, confronts us, insults us, teases us, etc., our emotional goal of feeling secure and significant is blocked, so we then choose a path to correct that person to reopen the path of our emotional goal. When your spouse disagrees with your parenting in front of your children, then your emotional goal of security or significance is blocked. Even if we outwardly disagree with them, inwardly, our negative emotions greatly increase as we try to reconcile the paradox between what that person thinks of us versus what we think of ourselves. This happens almost every time our spouses criticize our personality, our emotional responses, etc. Humans desire approval and acceptance from others. As a result, we then choose internal responses by continuing to argue with them in our minds, and/or disqualify them by insulting their character or judging their motives (fundamental attribution error). If we are successful, while we don't change their opinion of us, we do nullify the emotional impact of their opinion. We dismiss them in our minds and ignore their critique, which removes them as an obstacle to our emotional goal… to feel accepted and good about ourselves. Reflect on the stories you've told yourself about others over the years to achieve your emotional goals. Consider how many of these paths would pass the RHWR grid.

Likewise, we use various behavioral paths to procure our emotional goals. There are consistent times throughout the day when we want to feel differently than what we are currently feeling. We use food (cookies vs. fruits, vegetables, nuts), liquids (soda vs. water), various producers of dopamine (social media, video games), relationships (giving and asking affection from loved ones vs. inappropriate communication with the opposite sex), activities (accomplishing tasks vs. watching TV), and experiences (exercise vs. playing games). Choosing non-RHWR paths is the plight of the human experience, and soon, this choice becomes a habit. That leads us to an even greater battle: owning it. I'm assuming you thought I was going to say that the greatest battle was transitioning from a non-RHWR path to a path that is RHWR, which is certainly another great battle! But first, the greater tussle is owning the fact that the current path doesn't pass the RHWR test and truly being willing to change. Can we first let our defenses down and *openly* own the fact that our path is not RHWR?

My heart goes out to clients because many people find themselves pursuing emotional goals that originate from deep, profound hurt. Rejection, verbal, emotional, and physical abuse, trauma, neglect, and the like have created deep emotional holes in many hearts. Instead of pouring their energies into the micro emotional goals (day-to-day happiness and enjoyment), these individuals are desperately trying to climb out of the deeper and greater abyss of negative emotions and achieve the emotional goals of security, safety, trust, happiness, or belonging. Some could call this survival mode. They deeply want to solidify their emotional foundation so they can finally begin building and working on increasing their quality of life. Until then, they try to achieve the emotional goals of *not* feeling certain emotions (anxiety, stress, insecurities, etc.) through non-RHWR paths (drinking alcohol, spending too much time on social media and video games, flirting with someone who is not your spouse), which creates a downward spiral because these paths, while maybe offering temporary relief, creates more problems for them and for others around them.

A frequently used example of goal versus path is when someone experiencing a great deal of stress chooses the path of abusing alcohol to achieve the emotional goal of less stress/more peace. The emotional goal is good, but the path the person takes to achieve the emotional goal is unhealthy. Abusing alcohol to decrease negative emotions is one of the clearest examples of not only trying to achieve an emotional goal in a healthy way, but it also demonstrates the paradox of someone wanting to make an obvious change to their behavior (from non-RHWR paths to RHWR paths), but greatly struggling to do so. While the solution may seem obvious, many advise this person to just "stop." My approach to this individual would begin with first trusting that they truly do not want to use this path to help with the current stresses they are experiencing. Secondly, using the principle of goal/path theory, I would help them see that the goal isn't ultimately to quit drinking, but to reduce stress (emotional goal). When we only focus on the behavior, we may stop the behavior, but not deal with the core thing driving the behavior (the emotional goal). By doing this, we discuss several other paths they could use to achieve this same goal that would pass the test of rational, healthy, wise, and right. However, sometimes, even after equipping a person this way, they may still struggle to switch paths. Why? Is it because this person is not committed? Do they really want to change? I trust their motives, and frankly, I try very hard not to ever judge someone else's motives. I find it to be dangerous, offensive, and judgmental, and it doesn't help solve the problem. It's wasted energy. So then, what could the reason be why they are not switching paths?

It's crucial to understand that the non-RHWR paths have their own emotional rewards attached, and if we discontinue these paths, we will experience some kind of loss. In our example, when a person switches to a RHWR path from the non-RHWR path of drinking alcohol to relieve stress, they realize they must now forfeit the numbing (or even pleasant) feeling alcohol elicits. By switching paths, they encounter a type of emotional loss. Despite knowing the cost of abusing alcohol both physically, emotionally, and relationally, the numbing effects of alcohol may still hold them captive. Why? Because we all suffer from myopia. Myopia is simply a synonym for near-sightedness. We clearly see objects near us, but objects further away appear blurry. Symbolically, the emotional reward right in front of us is clear as crystal. Conversely, the consequences remain blurry or hidden. Since the positive feeling is "closer," we are more likely to go and grab it. The emotional intelligence (EI) skills that describe this process are *impulse control* and *delay of gratification*. We start to develop these skills from our very first breath. In infancy, we express our emotions and immediately start the goal/path process. We cry because we are hungry and want to feel full. However, sometimes, we cried just for attention, affirming our emotional goal of affection. This is one of the first big challenges for parents, who are responsible for developing the EI skills of impulse control and delayed gratification. If they know we don't have a need, they need to let us "cry it out" and control our impulses. If they don't succeed in this battle (because they have their own emotional goal: to feel comfort by comforting us), then they *enable* this non-RHWR behavior, prompting the baby to try it again. When we impulsively choose non-RHWR paths, we are setting a precedent for our future success, but also, we hurt those around us because they become obligated to respond to our choice. During the proverbial "terrible two's," we encounter the struggle of controlling our outbursts and impulse control, such as pushing our siblings or pinching our preschool friends. These proclivities follow us all the way through our challenging adolescent years. We struggle to restrain our impulses in relation to our teachers and parents, saying "no" to peer pressure and choosing to do homework and chores before watching TV or playing on our phones. I tell parents to use the phrase, "Duty and Discipline before Dopamine" as an easy reminder for their teens to memorize to start to train themselves in impulse control and delayed gratification.

These same lessons extend to college, learning how to have a successful relationship with a roommate or boyfriend/girlfriend, being able to communicate effectively with our spouses, and/or being consistent in exercising and eating healthy. We eventually develop impulse control and delayed gratification, or we would still be throwing temper tantrums on the ground and slapping people silly when we get angry with them. However, as with any skill, there are varying levels of skill development. Some are novices, some have a working knowledge, and others are masters. What is your skill level? The answer is given by your degree of success in stopping non-RHWR habits and forming new, RHWR habits. Controlling your impulse of wanting to continue to go back to the non-RHWR goals will help this stop-start process.

Security and Significance

Two main emotional goals impact our romantic relationships. Generally speaking, the main emotional goal for men is significance. Synonyms for significance are influence, prestige, relevance, and success. Generally speaking, the main emotional goal for women is security. Synonyms for security are safety, stability, steadiness, and sustainability. Even though I will process these two emotional goals in the context of romantic relationships, men and women tend to seek these emotional goals in every area of their lives. Secondly, while these emotional goals have more of a macro feel to them (quality of life), they are also ever-present in our micro situations (our spouse's affirmations vs. criticisms). One of the marriage books that has stood the test of time that I use with every couple I counsel is *His Needs, Her Needs* by Willard Harley[1]. He lists five main emotional needs for both men and women. I agree with the needs he lists, but I frame these needs as paths, not needs. Further, I don't call them needs; I call them wants. The explanation for this will be in my chapter on identity, value, and worth. A woman's main emotional goal is security. While there may be several paths for a woman to achieve this emotional goal, she wants her husband to take concrete, defined paths to help her achieve this emotional goal. These are: 1) affection, 2) intimate conversation, 3) honesty and openness, 4) financial support, and 5) family commitment. A man's main emotional goal is significance. While there may be several paths for a man to achieve this emotional goal, he wants

---

[1] Hartley, W. F. (1986). *His Needs, Her Needs* (Revised and Updated). Revell: Grand Rapids, MI

his wife to take very specific, defined paths to help him achieve the emotional goal of significance. These are: 1) admiration and appreciation, 2) sexual fulfillment, 3) physical attractiveness, 4) recreational companionship, and 5) domestic support.

If you are reading this book as a couple, it would be helpful to sit down and discuss these paths. You need to ask your spouse the very specific actions he or she wants within each pathway. For instance, a wife wants affection from her husband to achieve the emotional goal of security, but what are her favorite, most impactful ways to receive affection? Likewise, there are countless activities that can fall under recreational companionship, so ask your husband what specific activities he would love to do with you. Each of us have our specific preferences under each category, but I do want to expound on two of them, one for each partner. Guys, when it comes to intimate conversation, please don't make the mistake of thinking that intimate means sexual. I believe that the emotional goal a woman wants to achieve via this path that fulfills security is that she wants to *feel* that you "get" her better than anyone else gets her. The apex of this is when she feels you know her so well that she feels you get her even better than she gets herself, ***but she also feels she is completely safe with you as well***. Ladies, I believe the main path for a man to feel significant is admiration and appreciation, emphasizing admiration. Don't just compliment him but ***tell him how much it turns you on when you see him do something you appreciate***. I know the focus is always sex, but even for a guy, sex is empty for him unless he feels admired by you. However, when he feels admired by you, the sexual experience for him is mind-blowing. A woman *must* feel known and emotionally/relationally safe with her husband, and a husband *must* feel admired and have his sexual needs met. I will elaborate more on sexual intimacy later.

I also differentiate between emotional goals and paths when it comes to love languages. Another book that is probably even better known than *His Needs, Her Needs* is *The 5 Love Languages* by Gary Chapman[2]. These five love languages are 1) words of affirmation, 2) quality time, 3) receiving gifts, 4) acts of service, and 5) physical touch. Like *His Needs, Her Needs*, I believe these five love languages are specific pathways to achieving emotional goals. The main point Chapman is making is when we choose a path (an action) to have our partner *feel* love, we often choose the pathways we want our partner to choose in order for us to *feel* love. However, when we do this, the emotional goal is not achieved at all. Ask your partner which love languages they most like to receive. I have found that most men have words of affirmation and physical touch as their main ones (which should be evident in light of *His Needs, Her Needs*), and most women have quality time and one of the other ones as her top. However, I have heard some women say, "All five!" which actually makes it easier for her partner to achieve her emotional goal of love. Let me say that I have also seen men and women choose other ones as their main ones besides those I chose so as not to be too stereotypical! When you have the discussion on which languages rise to the top of the list for your partner, make sure you also get very specific details in *how* your partner can meet that love language.

---

[2] Chapman, G. D. (1992). *The 5 Love Languages: The Secret to Love that Lasts*. Northfield Publishing: Chicago, IL.

The Extreme Pain of Non-RHWR Sexual Paths

I have worked with many men and women who participate in certain sexual behaviors, whether it is promiscuity, pornography, emotional or physical affairs, etc., to achieve the emotional goals of security and significance. I will take an entire chapter to equip you on how to recover from these deep wounds, but for now, I want to use these behaviors to illustrate the difference between the emotional goals and paths we take to achieve those goals. These couples, who have been affected by immoral sexual behaviors, must overcome enormous obstacles in their healing process by first delving into their emotional goal and the path they chose to achieve it. I believe that no married person sets out to engage in immoral sexual behaviors intentionally, and it is often the result of a non-RHWR path taken to achieve an emotional goal. While a man may pour all his energy into his career or sports, most men's main path to significance is to be admired and desired by their girlfriends or wives. Seeking significance through a relationship with the opposite sex is a major factor leading up to men and immoral sexual behaviors. Like alcohol, there is an immediate reward, which can lead to disastrous consequences. Most women pursue a variety of paths to achieve the emotional goal of security (or safety). While most of the paths involve relationships with several friends and loved ones, the main path is through her relationship with her boyfriend or husband. Women fall into affairs when their husbands are not meeting the emotional goal of security through the pathways listed above in those popular books on marriage. Suppose her spouse doesn't meet one or more of these emotional goals, and someone else comes along and starts meeting her emotional goal via those specific pathways. An inappropriate emotional attachment may develop and may culminate sexually. The irony is many of these paths end up backfiring on the men and women who choose these non-RHWR paths, and when all is said and done, they are even farther away from their initial emotional goal.

The failure to meet one another's emotional goals doesn't just happen overnight. It may begin with what initially seemed like a healthy goal, which, over time, spiraled into an obsession. For men, it may be their careers, sports, or (believe it or not) video games, and for women, it could be their relationships with family, children, or friends. The failure to meet these emotional needs often lies in a lack of communication, either a lack of it or poor skills in problem resolution. Many problem-solving discussions escalate into arguments because we possess poor communication skills coupled with our own insecurities. We feel exposed and attacked. We defend ourselves while lashing out at our partner, and in the process, we hurt one another.

Anger towards your spouse or significant other usually stems from them speaking or doing something that increases your negative emotions. In other words, how they "made" you feel. Many men use the word "disrespected," while women describe feeling "emotionally unsafe." Anger is an attempt to get the other person to apologize and change how they come across to us so we no longer feel the threat to our emotional goal. The resulting emotion is typically not even from the disagreement but from *how* our spouse talks to us. Every couple has topics and problems they need to work through, but the reason why the emotions escalate so much is not because of our differing opinions but because of *the way* we disagree with one another gets interpreted as a threat to our security or significance. Therefore, we self-sabotage, using intensity, ridiculing, mocking their opinion, and insulting their character and motives. Brilliant... not. Now, because of their confrontation with us (whether it be *what* their criticism is or *how* they are communicating it), we see them obstructing our emotional goal and we use anger towards them as a way to remove them (via the same foolish paths) from blocking our emotional goals.

If the hurt continues and the anger persists, we begin to withdraw from one another, resulting in abandoning the emotional goals we vowed to each other at the altar. If this continues for a long enough period, each spouse may begin entertaining other paths to meet these emotional goals. Embarking on alternative paths can result in more criticism and anger. Women may start complaining about the video games, the golf, the friends, the job, and if she notices any relational engagement with a female "friend," the gloves come off. Because men are so dependent on being admired by the opposite sex, they fall more easily into sexual immorality. You ever wonder why it is throughout history that various men have had multiple wives while there isn't any pattern of women having multiple husbands? The lie is the greater number of women a man has desiring him, the greater he feels admired and desired, which then gets linked to the most addictive drug: sex. Our spouses are NEVER to blame for our immoral path choices, but if the path to our emotional goals is blocked, we foolishly make the mistake of trying to find other paths.

There is a verse in the Bible that says, "Remember, the sins of some people are obvious, leading them to certain judgment. But there are others whose sins will not be revealed until later (1 Timothy 5:24)."[3] Men are more easily exposed because they use outward, immoral sins (paths) to meet their emotional goals while women use more culturally acceptable paths to achieve their emotional goals. The immoral sexual behaviors are exposed and broadcast publicly, but only after much time, much counseling, and much healing do the sins of the wife become revealed. When I say sin, I mean her own mistakes in the marriage. Both are equally culpable for the state of their marriage, but only the man is culpable for the immoral behavior. Women rightly point out, "We are both to blame for the state of our marriage, but I never went outside of our marriage!" Because of this truth, it is difficult to transition the focus from the offense itself into what caused it: the failure to meet one another's needs.

Furthermore, even though the wife may not have turned to another man to meet her emotional needs, it doesn't necessarily mean the paths she used were more rational, healthy, wise, or right. Any alternate path we use to meet our marital emotional needs is not rational, healthy, wise, or right. We can't excuse ourselves by lamenting the fact that our spouses are not meeting our marital needs as justification for using those alternate paths. Using the paths discussed above may appear to be less offensive. However, this may make it more difficult for some women to acknowledge the need to make a change. Therefore, it's obviously easier to continue that path with little to no negative emotion (from consequences) motivating her back to the RHWR path of her husband. Think for a moment about the differences between pornography and romance novels.

---

[3] *Holy Bible*, New Living Translation, copyright © 1996, 2004, 2015 by Tyndale House Foundation.

The former is visual and offensive, but the latter can still be just as pornographic but in the form of "story" and relational romance. Is the social stigma attached to romance novels (or daytime dramas) lower than the social stigma attached to pornography? Both are still immoral, but you can see how 1 Timothy 5:24 is applied here.

All of the above examples are extreme, but I wanted to use extreme examples to create a stark contrast between very good emotional goals and how one can use non-RHWR paths to achieve these emotional goals. To help all of us grow, it should be obvious that we need to differentiate between the goals and the paths we take to achieve those goals. The key to learning is repetition: everything we do is an attempt to meet an emotional goal; the emotional goal is good; we need to evaluate the path through the RHWR grid. Framed this way, this is what you must do:

1. List the non-RHWR behaviors you want to change.
2. Name the emotional goal(s) you are trying to achieve by that behavior (path).
3. List several RHWR paths (behaviors) you can choose to accomplish the same goal.
4. Name the emotional reward you will lose by switching paths. Grieve the loss, agree with the loss, and accept the loss.
5. Fight, fail, recover, and succeed in adopting other RHWR paths. "For a righteous man may fall seven times and rise again, but the wicked shall fall by calamity." (Proverbs 24:16)[4]

---

[4] The Holy Bible, New King James Version, Copyright © 1982 Thomas Nelson.

CHAPTER 2:

BLIND TO WHAT YOU CANNOT SEE

Many waters cannot quench love, nor can the floods drown it . . .

Song of Songs 8:7

Our Mental Model

The paths we choose to achieve our micro and macro emotional goals come from our way of thinking, mindset, or mental models. Our mental model is the organic (ever-changing) product of 1) all the stored information we have in our brains and 2) the formulas we use to process that information. Our DNA, life experiences, and choices form our formulas. DNA dictates all physical traits. Within our DNA are the foundational formulas for our IQ, outward appearance, medical elements (like Autism or genetic disorders), as well as our personality/temperament. Besides the formation of our bodies, our gender also impacts the formulas of thinking in our brains. A boy fetus will get a surge of testosterone that changes his body, but when his brain receives this testosterone, I describe it as "frying" some of the connections between the two hemispheres of the brain, called the *corpus callosum*. This results in the male brain creating a greater distinction between facts and emotions. There are several books on this topic, so I won't go into exhaustive detail other than to say I describe the male brain as a hallway and the female brain as a gym. The male goes into separate rooms, which means he can focus on one thing and one thing only while blocking out all the other areas of his life. Women have all topics networked together and can "feel" all the areas of their lives at once. There are strengths and weaknesses to the way both male and female brain's function. The strength of a woman's brain is that everything she processes must run through her emotional center. The foolish way to frame it is that women are *too* emotional when in fact, it is the processing of emotions that determines one's level of maturity. This is why we say men can be childish and ineffective in relationships. However, the strength of a man is his ability to separate facts from emotions, which is effective when the speed of decision making is paramount and when a complex problem needs to be boiled down to limited choices.

I hear husbands often complain that their wives will bring up a frustration, but after much discussion, wasn't the real issue. When she voices concerns about his activities (hanging out with friends, sports, video games, etc.), he assumes it's the activity itself that's the issue, but she simply wants more time with him and sees his attention to the activity as a barrier. Often, she brings up a topic that "triggers" her, tied to an unmet emotional need, but ends up discussing the topic rather than the need. Men often miss this underlying need, focusing instead on defending their activities. Can I get a witness? The takeaway is that we're born with certain relationship patterns but rarely taught how to refine them. To navigate life more effectively, we must adapt these instinctive responses.

As we execute our proactive and reactive response formulas, we store the results of each experience and deem them either good or bad, successful or unsuccessful, neutral, confusing or troubling, or a mixture of all of the above. Our life experiences impact, mold, and change how we see the world, view ourselves, and pursue our goals. DNA combined with lived experiences shape our unconscious mental model, embedding all the data we've gathered along with the formulas we use to process each moment. This model reflects our quality of life, worldview, and sense of self in the world.

The final component that regularly morphs our formulas is choice. We make a choice and experience the results of that choice, good or bad, and our mental model stores that data. It may seem as if the process is solid and should result in a higher success rate, but alas, it does not (or else you wouldn't be reading this book). What is the issue? The most obvious answer is that at any one moment, we lack all the information or the correct information to make the best decision. Secondly, our interpretation formulas can be way off, producing a wrong decision. Thirdly, we do not incorporate all the variables of the situation or put too much or too little emphasis on each variable. Considering these three possible causes, the potential for mistakes is high. Long ago, I determined that my mental model was faulty and learned not to trust it. Surprisingly, some of us may have way too much faith and trust in our mental models and dismiss any thought that our current way of thinking may be flawed. We are always seeking and exploring new information, which is great. However, new information and insights combined with inaccurate formulas (ways of using that information in decision-making) will still produce a poor product. Some of us run, avoid, ignore, or even suppress negative emotions because we don't want to face the fact that our thinking is way off. Even if we know it internally, we don't want to own it, and we get defensive if someone points it out. Let's unpack this further.

Should Be or Not Should Be, that is the Question

As you can easily see, is the way our mental model operates is incredibly organic, constantly changing and morphing. The growth and development of our thinking happens naturally and automatically throughout our lives, which is both passive (and active) in nature. The passive process occurs in our subconscious and the unconscious (DNA/previous life experiences), while the active process occurs in the conscious (free will). The most effective approach is to actively assess and evaluate the status quo in these areas, identifying necessary changes for greater success. While this seems obvious, many people impulsively accept their mental model's suggestions without questioning their validity. I named my business "Becoming More" because my goal is to equip people in the ongoing process (hence the continuing and ongoing form of "become") to become as successful as they can be. Success can mean alleviating the current negative emotions that have become an impediment to their everyday life experience (by means of counseling), or they are doing well and want to become *more* successful and *more* effective in their role as a leader, parent, spouse, God-follower, etc. My tagline is: *Everyone becomes what they want to; only some people think about becoming more.* The "want" is defined as blindly accepting the suggestions of your mental model without challenge. Because your mental model suggests it, you naturally want to trust it. If your mental model suggests you hit the snooze button several times in the morning, order another drink at the bar, or tell your boss exactly what you think of him, that is what you *want* to do. Every human being does this, but some of us pause, evaluate what our mental model is proposing, and say in their conscious mind, "Wait, that is really dumb." The pause starts the process of reprogramming our mental model to become *more* effective and successful. This is not just a mechanical process of *think, feel*, and *do*, trying to achieve micro and macro emotional goals. It is also a deeper evaluation of our *beliefs, opinions, convictions, values, and overall philosophy of life*. Where did you get these beliefs, opinions, convictions, values, and overall philosophy of life? Did you form them on your own, or did they come from outside of you? Are there universal moral truths, values, and convictions? If so, then objective truth exists, and there is a source for this objective truth, namely God.

Mental Model Formula Formation: Grace and empathy without truth and boundaries is enablement. Truth and boundaries without grace and empathy are toxic.

What if our opinion of ourselves doesn't need to change, but there are others in our life who believe we need to change in one way? Do we automatically agree, or do we automatically dismiss and ignore? If we are totally honest, there are areas of our lives that we don't think should change, but, in all reality, they should (such as some of our personal habits). Wait. Who determined it should change? Why do I have to be the one to change? If their opinion is wrong, they are the ones who need to change, right? Before evaluating yourself, look at people in your own life. It's easier to look objectively at others for objective truth because we can be defensive about our weaknesses, failings, etc. Here's what I recommend. Instead of trying to apply the principle to ourselves (as that may produce negative emotions), we should step back and apply the other principle first. Then, we can objectively arrive at wisdom and truth, then apply it to ourselves.

Bless Their Heart

Have you ever had the following thought about another human being, "Wow, they don't get it. They are so defensive and don't even realize it hurts both them and others around them. They are so blind"? I spent most of my life in Michigan and always loved hearing about Southern hospitality. So, when I moved to Texas, I experienced that genuine Southern hospitality firsthand. I found that Southerners have much in common with our kin in England because they both are known to have a tongue-in-cheek approach to relationships. "Bless your heart" is a common saying here and disguised as a form of Southern hospitality. In reality, it is a back-handed way of saying, "You're clueless and just don't get it, honey." We can probably name someone like this and honestly know we are right in our assessments. Sometimes it is a combination. Some people acknowledge the validity of a particular behavior needing to be on the list but are completely blind as to the degree of the issue.

They say, "Yeah, I know I need to work on that," and we say to ourselves, "But you have no clue how bad it is." Despite agreeing with the item, there is no real effort or urgency in addressing it. Now, bring it back into the subjective realm and *be open to the idea that you may come to someone's mind if they were to think of someone who doesn't "get it."* Hopefully, at this point, it is apparent that we need help from others to gain insight into how and why we must change.

The Johari Window and the Eradication of the Blind Area

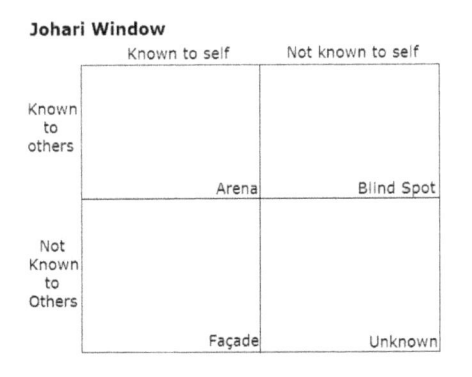

Johari Window

	Known to self	Not known to self
Known to others	Arena	Blind Spot
Not Known to Others	Façade	Unknown

The Johari Window Model is a technique produced by two psychologists, Joseph Luft and Harrington Ingham (Joe and Harry combined to become Johari), in 1955. The overall goal is to help people better understand themselves and their relationships. The model is described as a window because there are four boxes joined together to form a "window." The four windows are labeled Arena/Open, Façade/Hidden, Blind, and Unknown.

Information that is easily known to other people and known to self is the Arena/Open area. I've already disclosed to you that I was a pastor, counselor, coach and consultant, and professor. That is my "open" information that you know, and I know. Then there is information about myself that is known to me but not known to you.

That is the Façade/Closed area. This means there is information that I want to remain hidden and unknown to the world. We all have a closed area containing many truths and facts about our lives. Why? Because we are fearful. We are all scared. If other people knew that information about us, we believe they would think less of us and possibly tell other people, which would influence other people to think less about us. The creators call it the Façade area because we create a façade when we try to influence what other people think about us by withholding certain information from them. We all choose what information we are willing to move from the Closed area to the Open area and to whom we reveal this information.

Going Deeper into the Closed Area (Foreshadowing of a Source of Negative Emotions)

You will notice a consistent practice I use throughout this book. Whenever I discuss concepts that refer to a human being resisting in some way, shape, or form doing something that is good and healthy, I want to step back and examine what the motivation or goal may be behind their actions. Yes, revealing information in the Closed area would expose information that others could use against us and hurt us. What bad happens if we revealed information in the Closed area? But what bad happens if this information remains hidden? What good happens if this information comes to light? What good happens if this information stays closed? Each piece of information produces different answers. If we truly have the desire to grow, mature, and improve who we are at the deepest level of our souls, there is some information that we absolutely need to reveal.

Even though we know this to be true, we still hesitate to share this information out of the fear that it may damage some relationships. To illustrate, I'll use one of the best verses that describe who Jesus Christ is and how He interacts with all of us. You will notice the same words from the formula formation principle above. John 1:14 states, "The Word became flesh and made his dwelling among us. We have seen his glory, the glory of the one and only Son, who came from the Father, *full of grace and truth.*" The last phrase is the focus of my point. Throughout the gospels, when we read about each interaction Jesus had with people, His statements were graceful and empathic. He spoke the truth, addressing where people were wrong and needed to change. Anyone who reads the gospels can't walk away and criticize Jesus's approach to people. He achieved both goals (grace and truth) with each individual or group. The only people He gave truth to, with a great deal of intensity, were the people who wouldn't admit they were blind, refused to own anything, and were opposed to being open to correction. Interesting.

Describing Jesus, or God, as full of grace and truth is a theological and philosophical concept that is far-reaching and has profound depths of knowledge, insight, and understanding that one cannot fully understand in terms of meaning and impact. But if we keep it on the surface and apply it to interpersonal relationships, it becomes an extremely effective principle. As I (just like you) form relationships, I share general information about myself. When the other person receives the information positively (with empathy and grace), I feel safe and confident to share more truth about myself. Relationships grow and deepen if grace continues as we reveal more truth. At some point in the relationship, permission to speak the truth is either asked for or granted because enough grace has been experienced, achieving emotional safety. Thus, one can comfortably share more truth. What happens when we receive judgement for the truth we share? At that point, the sharing of further information on a deeper level ceases and becomes officially locked within the Closed Area of the Johari Window because we no longer feel safe. Think of your closest relationships and evaluate why you haven't shared more details about yourself. It very well may be because you are convinced, correctly or incorrectly, that you won't receive grace. When someone knows something intimate about us and their reaction lacks grace and empathy, it feels toxic.

Today, we see how the push for tolerance, under the guise of empathy, has been exaggerated to an extreme. Don't misunderstand—empathy is essential when balanced with grace and truth, but anything taken to an extreme becomes a weakness. I believe many now err on the side of empathy and sympathy to avoid being called toxic. In addition, many may be motivated by their own desire to avoid negative emotions and the desire of acceptance over the necessities of truth and boundaries on behaviors. The result is irresponsible enablement. Wisdom dictates that in every relationship (especially marital and familial relationships), both goals need to be always achieved. I often advise clients when they need to be truthful with a loved one in their life, they make a statement of grace, love, and empathy, such as "I love you and am committed to you." Then, they share the truth, "What you are doing is not RHWR, and you need to really consider changing." Then followed by another statement of grace, "I am for you and committed to you. I love you."

The Hidden and Blind Areas of the Johari Window

The area that is not known to you or me is the Hidden area. Here are the aspects about myself that I don't even know, and, of course, if I don't know them, neither do you. It's simply hidden, and shedding light on this area is often a lifelong process of growth and discovery. It involves the deepest of self-reflections and obtaining the most profound of insights. Here we basically find our meaning, our identity, our purpose, etc. I hope that by reading this book, the journey becomes more tangible so that you can become more strategic in achieving the macro goal of increasing your quality of life.

The final area, the area that has caused me the greatest amount of dismay, fear, and trepidation, is the fourth area of the Johari Window, called the Blind area. The Blind area is the area that I don't see about myself, *but you do*. Just the thought alone that other people see things about me that I don't see about myself gives me a reason to pause. On the flip side, there are certain areas, aspects, details of my life, my personality, my gifts, skills, and abilities that others see that I don't and that can be *positive*. Most of us are self-critical, underestimate our own value, and need others to give us these objective truths so that we can be more successful. When it comes to areas of my life that are positive and encouraging, I want to be aware of those areas and accept them as gifts.

The greater endeavor, of course, is to unveil the areas that we don't see about ourselves that others see as negative. I have already encouraged you to think of people throughout your life who may have a blind area you desperately wish they would see. So, doesn't it logically stand to reason that you may possess areas of your life of which you may be unaware and others may greatly wish you could see? The only way for you to avoid being the "their" in "bless their heart" is if someone chooses to be brave and share with you the truth. But wouldn't doing so risk the relationship? My question is: if it is indeed your issue and not theirs, why would they struggle to tell you? Your blindness is your issue, especially if it's causing pain to others. It's not their responsibility to tell you; it's your responsibility to inquire as to what it may be. It is each of our responsibilities to grow and mature in order to add value to other's lives. Having negative traits that hurt others or create a negative atmosphere is not someone else's responsibility; it is our job to objectively evaluate it and ask ourselves if we see traits in others that need to change. We often believe that when someone gets up the nerve to confront us about an offensive aspect of our personality, we feel they are the only person who feels that way. There is one way to find out: proactively ask other people in your life if they feel the same way. Don't assume it's just that one person's issue. Do you think there might be a gap between your subjective view of yourself and the objective view of yourself that others hold? How are you going to close that gap?

The Beginning of the Objective/Subjective Process of View of Self

My work, whether as a pastor, counselor, director, professor, coach, or consultant, has focused on guiding others to prioritize objective truth over subjective experience and eliminate blind spots. Objective truth comes from external sources: our parents, our family, our friends, society, culture, and the like. In addition, and most importantly, objective truth comes from God. What every religion has in common are commitments to morality, selflessness, and the pursuit of wisdom. Anyone or anything that influences our lives suggests items they believe should be included in our personal growth and development plan (our point B). We first determine whether we agree to adopt or dismiss that opinion. If we agree with it, adding it to our list only creates more distance from point A to point B. Even if we disagree with it, we will experience tension because of the paradox between what is and what should be. We burn copious amounts of emotional energy trying to reconcile the disconnect between what others believe about us and what we believe about ourselves. Even if we agree, we are less motivated to do those things because they aren't produced from within us.

However, you now know that there are new areas in your personal development plan (point B) that you must incorporate outside of yourself because it is true and objective. Though it can be painful, you must create a strategy to turn unreached goals into a new status quo, making them a true part of who you are. To be sure, don't think that the two lists in point B are entirely separate because many of the items do overlap. Many suggestions we receive from objective sources (others' objective, truthful opinions of you) and objective truth (the Lord), were already in either the Open or Closed areas of our Johari Window. It is the Blind area you must uncover and move into the light. As illustrated in the mental model section, we must be in a constant search for that objective truth. All of us have experienced objective opinions that do not align with objective truth, which makes us cautious when we hear those objective opinions. However, we must be just as cautious when we receive subjective opinions from our mental models. The goal is to search and receive objective truth and form our mental models to what is RHWR, regardless of the source.

Societal Objective Truth

I think we can all agree on the need for laws in our society; otherwise, it would be anarchy. We understand that these laws are necessary because disobeying them would harm others, as well as ourselves. Have you considered the fact that every law in society has some tie to morality? There isn't one law in society, not one, that doesn't have morality attached to it. I remember sitting in my government class in 9th grade, and the topic was the Prohibition Era in America. My teacher asked us at the conclusion of the discussion: what the ultimate reason was for Prohibition's failure? He proceeded to answer his own question, "Because you can't make laws against people's morals." Something in me sprung up, and I immediately raised my hand (I didn't give him an opportunity to call on me) and proclaimed, "What law exists that is not based on morals?" He didn't respond. Every law is rooted in morality, where individuality is secondary to protecting the rights of others first and then themselves. Even speed limits exist because objective truth states that if the primary emotional goal in determining driving laws were individuality and autonomy-driven (excuse the pun), the consequences would be catastrophic, right? I am pounding the point that the only way to have a successful society is for all of us to submit to objective truth standards like RHWR, not only on a macro, societal level, but all the way down to our micro, personal level in the formation of who we are as people.

Not Just Openness to, but Obsession with, Objective Truth

There are copious Scriptures, along with John 1:14 (Jesus came full of grace and truth), that have been foundational in forming the basic theories in my career. In Proverbs, it states that the goal is to search for wisdom, knowledge, and understanding as if it is literally hidden treasure. Proverbs 2:1-11 states:

My son, if you accept my words
  and store up my commands within you,
2 turning your ear to wisdom
  and applying your heart to understanding—
3 indeed, if you call out for insight
  and cry aloud for understanding,
4 and if you look for it as for silver
  and search for it as for hidden treasure,
5 then you will understand the fear of the Lord
  and find the knowledge of God.
6 For the Lord gives wisdom;
  from his mouth come knowledge and understanding.
7 He holds success in store for the upright,
  he is a shield to those whose walk is blameless,
8 for he guards the course of the just
  and protects the way of his faithful ones.
9 Then you will understand what is right and just
  and fair—every good path.

10 For wisdom will enter your heart,
   and knowledge will be pleasant to your soul.
11 Discretion will protect you,
   and understanding will guard you.

There are several points I want to make. Firstly, if you must search for something, you have yet to find it and, therefore, do not possess it. Secondly, notice the intensity and desperation by which we are to search for knowledge, insight, wisdom, and understanding. We "turn our ear to it," meaning we are open to it. Next, it states we are to "call out for it" and "cry aloud for it" and to "search for it as if it were a hidden treasure." Think of all the things in life right now you are the most desperate to obtain. We cry out for a solution to our finances, to the pain in our marriage, the suffering of being under a poor leader at work, etc., but we should also be crying out for insight, wisdom, and understanding. To summarize a major proposition of this book, we must first understand how we may be blind in many areas, grasp the fact that our mental models produce suggestions and conclusions that should be evaluated, and seek insight and wisdom revealing to us exactly the areas we are blind. These safeguards will help improve our thinking "formulas" and equip us with more effective responses.

Be warned that the information we discover in wisdom, knowledge, and understanding, we may not initially agree with and want to reject. Therein lies the battle of humanity because the truths in wisdom, knowledge, and understanding are often found in our blind areas and therefore difficult to obtain. And quite honestly, incorporating those truths and processes can be painful. Unfortunately, we all know relationships where the refusal of, agreement with, and adoption of these objective truths is lifelong and, even more sadly, has yet to be achieved. I do find many people open and desirous of this type of insight; however, many fail to follow through with the intensity required to discover this insight by exposing themselves emotionally to apply the necessary insights.

Equipping: The Habit of Proactive Teachability

Teachability can, in many ways, be likened to humility, which is considering other people over yourself. I promote using the word "teachability" over the word "humility" because some misinterpret the term by believing it is the practice of diminishing their value and worth. Humility is a complex heart issue. Conversely, teachability is simply an attribute that means we know we don't know everything and are open to learning from others. Teachability and humility are the opposite of pride. What is the practical definition of pride? Pride is a dismissive response to environmental opinions. Pride is when the person concludes they already have all the information/data they need in their mental models. Not only that, but they also have the most effective formulas and critical thinking to automatically produce the right opinions and conclusions. Frankly put, they don't need your insight. To be fully transparent, I struggle to have patience with these people, but I must remember that I truly believe at the core of that mindset is a deep vacuum of value and worth. They default to an automatic pride response because it's too painful for them to go through the process of exposing these deep insecurities.

On the contrary, teachable people are open to and desirous of information that they don't possess, and secondly, they are open to and desirous of new ways of thinking and processing. When teachable people encounter new information, they can now process it with a new formula or way of thinking or a new set of eyes that they didn't have before. Those of us who remember taking Algebra know that in a formula, if the x^2 should be an x^3, the product of the formula will be wrong. Just as in our mental model process, wrong formulas mean incorrect interpretations (biases, assumptions, etc.).

Now let's combine the philosophy of Proverbs 2 with the concept of teachability. I would say most of us only practice *reactive* teachability. What does that mean? Reactive teachability is how we react when someone builds up the courage to point out the fact that we are lacking information or, more difficult yet, have an incorrect way of thinking. They are nervous to start a conflict because addressing a legitimate issue may result in the person feeling unsafe or exposed. Some have no hesitancy in calling out blind spots, but most hesitate and avoid it out of fear of conflict. Either way, reactive teachability is when people come into our lives and tell us that we need to be corrected in some way, in a grace-and-truth way. Those who are truly teachable have no problem with that. In fact, we invite the insight because we're open to and desirous of that change. We understand that we may have blind areas and want them to eradicate them. Isn't that a healthy goal? So, ultimately, maturity and teachability are essential in minimizing and shrinking the three areas of our Closed, Hidden, and Blind boxes within the Johari Window. The result is an expansion of our open areas, leading to true life fulfillment.

We can never arrive at fulfillment with reactive teachability alone. Why? Reactive teachability is rarely effective because everyone naturally resists these confrontations out of fear it will result in defensiveness or an attack. To be the most effective in eradicating the Closed, Hidden, and Blind areas, we must do more than reactive teachability, hoping and waiting for others to build up the courage to come to us. To accomplish this, we must practice *proactive* teachability. It is the RHWR path of regularly going to people in your life and asking them the hard questions: "Where am I blind? How can I grow? How can I be better?" But even if we do this, some may still be hesitant to be completely honest out of the same fear of conflict. You must, therefore, "pull" it out of them. After asking these questions, follow up by saying, "I'm not looking for the obvious information, I want the information in the back of your mind that you would never share with me. That is the information I need for two reasons; first, I may be blind to that information and am desperate to gain insight, wisdom, knowledge, and understanding. The second reason is that you may have information or an opinion or conclusion about me that may be incorrect because of some misunderstanding or experience, and I would love the opportunity to correct that."

If you feel that this is too extreme, then what other paths can you come up with to get true feedback from others and fulfill the principle of Proverbs 2? Considering the application of this technique, is there anyone you know, perhaps even yourself, who *desperately* needs to practice proactive teachability? As a matter of fact, shouldn't every human being practice this? Imagine what our world would be like. Even if you don't receive any new information from the person, or the information they offer is faulty, think about the transformational impact on each of you through this exercise.

What if you practiced this at work? What if you practiced this with your family?

I often ask my clients questions like, "Are you a good wife?" "Are you a good husband?" Often, their answers can be quite humorous. Without even thinking, they may reply, "Well, there are different areas I need to improve, but yeah, I think so." I would then ask, "Have you ever asked your wife if you're good husband?" or "Have you ever asked your husband if you're a good wife?" Shouldn't our spouses have a major say in whether we are a good spouse? Then why haven't we asked them? Are you a good parent? Are you a good listener? Are you a good boss? Have you ever asked the people you are listening to if they feel heard by you? Have you ever asked your children how you can improve as a parent? (You may be surprised by their answers). Have you ever asked your followers if you are a good leader? There's no need to feel defensive as to why you haven't or wouldn't; just ask them. It's not as if they hold the monopoly on the objective truth in each of these respective roles, but they absolutely may have information about you that you don't possess about yourself (the good ole blind area). Remember, the bonus in doing this is also building relationships based on your humility, teachability, and transparency. These are incredibly powerful human traits people admire and have the impact of motivating and convicting others to do the same.

Summary

Our mental models are an accumulation of a vast amount of information we have gathered throughout our lives, including the numerous formulas we use in interpreting and responding to every situation. These formulas stem from our DNA, life experiences, and choices. As we live, our mental models constantly change as we gain information and learn how to be more successful in accomplishing our micro (here-and-now) and macro (quality of life/standard of living) emotional goals. However, our philosophy of life, comprised of our convictions, values, and beliefs about morality, also impacts and helps to form our quality of life. The admission that our mental model may be flawed in more ways than we may be aware of and may consist of numerous blind spots is essential to our mental health and relationships. As we apply the RHWR grid to the paths we use to achieve our micro and macro emotional goals, we must also do the same with our philosophy of life. The only way for this to be truly successful is to be obsessed with eradicating our blind areas and instead be consumed with gaining more insight, wisdom, and understanding. If you are ready, let's open that door together and walk the path toward gaining insight, wisdom, and understanding, unlocking the power of our negative emotions.

CHAPTER 3:

OUR EMOTIONAL STORMS

Do not stir up nor awaken love until it pleases. – Song of Songs 2:7

This will be the last *foundational* chapter carried over from my first book, I^3. I believe laying this foundation is crucial in both books because the application overlap is too important to miss in case you only read this book. For your information, what is missing in this book that is in my first book is the deeper dive into the main negative emotions of anxiety, fear, worry, anger, and depression, the chapter on how to solidify your identity value and worth, and the chapter outlining my process for helping clients heal from trauma. However, I did include the chapters on insecurity and my technique of I^3: Information, Interpretation, and Intensity because the negative emotion of insecurity contains the doorway to us truly facing our negative emotions (and, um, because of the title and subtitle of this book). My main premise of both books is the truth that walking into our negative emotions is our most effective pathway for growth, healing, maturity, and obtaining the ever-coveted state of rest and peace. Finally, if each of you needs to do some personal work on those negative emotions or your identity, value, worth, and/or trauma, then walking through the process in my first book is crucial. Why? Because your spouse is not responsible for your response to your negative emotions. He or she may trigger you, but the *amount* of your negative emotions and the solution to your negative emotions rests entirely with you, not them. My goal is to empower you with the ability to remove any and all control of your negative emotions from the environment and place it within the core of your heart. To do so, you may have to face some truths you have been avoiding up until now. Like Morpheus told Neo in the famous movie *The Matrix*, "There's a difference between knowing the path, and walking the path."

The Three Foundational Tenets of Daily Emotional Management

Clients reach out to me because their negative emotions get in the way of their lives. They need help managing their negative emotions. While there are several negative emotions, I use the main emotions of insecurity, anxiety, fear, worry, anger, and depression. To equip them fully, we must address two additional concepts that impact their daily emotional management, namely their identity, value, and worth, and the trauma they experienced. I use the word trauma in a general sense, not diagnostically. Any negative experience where healing is needed, I classify as trauma in light of the fact the emotional impact of those negative experiences carries over to several future situations until healing takes place. In each of these areas, we feel a different degree of loss, and we need to recognize it as loss, which gives us permission to grieve. With grieving, there is nothing to fix; we just need to give ourselves permission to hurt. With the surface emotions of insecurity, anxiety, fear, worry, anger, and/or depression, there is an *emotional loss of the moment*. When we get hit with any negative experience and take it personally, there is a *loss of our* worth. Finally, when we experience the immense pain of trauma, there is a *loss to a part of our soul*. Recognize it as loss; it's okay to hurt. Now, before I start walking through how to emotionally manage negative emotions, I want to establish three foundational tenets.

Tenet One: Emotion is Energy

First, *emotion is energy*. I frame emotion this way because I believe emotion is the energy we use to act, but also, I have found that many people have a difficult time accurately labeling and assessing the murkiness of their emotions and how to manage them. When we label emotions as energy, we can more easily assess, understand, evaluate, and correct it. From this perspective, I say there is good emotion/energy and negative (not bad) emotion/energy. The good energy is the excitement energy we burn to improve our micro and macro quality of life, which creates greater positive emotions. Negative, again, not bad; emotion/energy is just simply the energy produced in the process of problem-solving. Think of it this way: I have a problem, I'm creating negative consequences, and I want it fixed and want it to go away. Maybe I have a paper to write, I am out of clean underwear, or I'm in an argument with my loved one. Whatever it is, it produces negative energy, and that energy is there to ensure that the problem gets solved. Issues arise when we have too much of either kind of emotion. Too much good energy is overstimulation or addiction to good emotion, such as avoiding responsibilities or creating too much dopamine with video games, entertainment, or substance abuse. Too much negative emotion can be debilitating anxiety, depression, rage, or stress.

The Second Tenet: The Type and Amount of Emotional Energy

Next comes the second tenant, which is the need to correctly label the type of negative emotion, as well as having the right *amount* of emotional energy. Using a scale of one to ten, how much emotional energy does my present situation need? This is determined by evaluating our behavioral response and the energy required for it. Energy is literal physical energy burned in the verbal, nonverbal, or response of action. Having a "10" level of emotional energy is not automatically bad because the amount of energy needed is objectively based on each specific situation. For example, when we heard the news that we were going to be first-time grandparents, our positive energy skyrocketed. It is a joy that only those who get that news truly understand. We cannot wait to spoil that child and hand them back to their parents. Yep, and that's the way it should be, deal with it. If the amount of positive emotional energy stayed at the level when we first heard the news, we would turn into "helicopter" grandparents, and our children would rightfully avoid us like the plague. Conversely, if at some point our grandchild runs out into the street (because, of course, his parents weren't watching him, hence our need to be helicopters), I assess the situation and ask myself, "Hmm, how much energy do I need to address the situation?" That evaluation happens in a millisecond, and I leap with a "10" level to protect my grandchild. The level of energy needed is based upon either the degree of good news I hear or the degree of danger or negative consequences that could result from the situation.

Our Emotional Storms

While it is most common for us to experience an inflation of negative emotion, there are times when the emotional energy is too low, such as a teenager's level of emotional energy when it comes to completing their homework or chores or when a spouse is too passive in romantically pursuing their spouse. The goal is to have the right amount of emotion and energy. People reach out to me because they are troubled by their current status quo, and most of the time, they would define their status quo as suffering from an overwhelming amount of negative emotional energy. There are several reasons why they carry this weight. They either avoid the very action that would burn off the emotional energy, or, more commonly, the amount of their emotional energy is way too high for the areas of their life they attribute to causing the emotional energy in the first place. Most situations may only need a two or three on the scale of importance, but they have a six, seven, or eight level of energy. Even if they did respond effectively, the situation, by definition, can only objectively absorb a two or three amount of energy, so they still "carry" the rest of the energy. More frequently, they unleash all six to eight points of energy on the poor situation (normally a person) and cause damage in some way. We all know what it feels like to both dump that extra energy as well as have that negative energy dumped on us. It's not a pleasant experience. After this dumping, we then have a whole new problem situation on our hands, producing an entirely new package of energy that needs to be burned to recover from the damage caused by the first mistake. This is a very cyclical process and often doesn't get resolved. We get burned out dealing with it and just resign ourselves that it won't get solved, but the negative energy sits inside of us, rotting, until we find a way to solve it or heal from the overall experience.

Causes of the Emotional Storms

While there may be multiple reasons for the exorbitant amount of emotional energy, I believe there are three main causes. Before I delve into the causes, allow me to lay out another key premise. *Emotions don't produce themselves; they come from sentences in our minds.* Those sentences are thoughts and opinions about us, the situation, and the people involved. These statements create the energy based on the experience at hand or what needs to change to create a different experience. These formulas in our mental model fill in all the variables, calculate how to interpret them, and evaluate all the potential outcomes, giving a weight of importance to those outcomes, which produces our emotional energy. The emotional energy is then burned through the expression of joy (if positive emotional energy), or through some action response (if negative emotional energy) to change the status quo of the situation. This process itself is natural. As stated, the problem is not the existence of negative emotions. It is when the emotional energy does not match the objective intensity of the situation. There are three main causes for this inflation of emotion. First, there is some form of a lie we believe about the situation. If we are looking for a job, for example, we may believe the lie and say to ourselves, "I'll never get a job!" If we are having a difficult time in a relationship, we insert lies about the other person, wrongly judging their motives for example, or believe lies about ourselves such as "I'm an idiot, I ruined the relationship." The various interpretations motivate us to choose certain paths. We choose non-RHWR paths because we believe these lies about the situation. Even if we are practicing impulse control and successfully choose an RHWR path, the inflated negative energy doesn't dissipate, keeping us escalated. Why? Where do you burn emotional energy to solve a lie? The only way to reject it is by replacing it with statements that are true. For example, if I believe I'll never get a job, I will replace it with statements of truth, such as, "The truth is I did not try as hard as I should have in high school and college, so I don't qualify for the jobs I want. However, I could finish college or go to trade school, and if I work hard in any job, I can get promoted. I just may have to accept a job I don't want now to eventually get the job I do want." The goal is not to replace lies with positive – but true – statements. I am all about giving and providing hope and encouragement, but it must be based on truth. I would love to say to myself, "I am the greatest golfer in the world." It certainly is positive, but it isn't true. Jesus said that the truth would set you free (John 8:32), not positive, motivational statements. However, you can make positive emotional statements to yourself that would be effective, such as, "I will be confident. I am tenacious. I will be successful." Then, form your mental model strategy based on truth to get you there!

I have also observed another emotionally damaging trend among clients. Clients could process a story objectively and truthfully, but they end with either a question or a statement that isn't true or provable, and it has the same negative effect of creating a large amount of negative emotion that has no outlet. I have a client who struggles with anxiety about her health and the health of her family. She had a mammogram, and her doctor told her it came back clear. She concluded, "But what if he's wrong?" Her mind concluded the story of her mammogram with a question that produced doubt, to which her mental model then responded logically with a great deal of anxiety and fear. I asked her to answer her own question with truth, *i.e. is he wrong?* Another client processed a situation and then concluded with, "I don't think I had integrity in that situation." In this case, it wasn't a question but a conclusion where she judged herself. I advised her to "prove" to me that she didn't have integrity. Whenever we make character evaluations about ourselves or others that aren't action-based but an overall evaluation based on a series of behaviors, we conjure up stories in our minds that we use to back up the claim. However, we need to prove that all those statements or examples are either true or RHWR. Even if this client was correct, she still needs to be as specific as possible about where her integrity fell short so she can burn her emotional energy on a specific strategy to rectify it or grow from it. The other point is that she may have made a mistake, but it isn't an issue of integrity. Or, she may be wrong altogether, and she couldn't have responded any better. Truth is the goal, because it produces the right words to describe it and produces the right amount of emotional energy because it is the product of an action strategy to respond to the true statements, opinions, and conclusions about the topic at hand.

Mental Model Formula Formation: Build self-awareness of what sentences of interpretation your mental model is producing and replace all lies with truth.

The second major cause of the emotional storms is related to our Identity, Value, and Worth (IVW). I will take an entire chapter to walk through the formation of our IVW and how to take control of it. But for the sake of my point, I will simply say that our emotion gets inflated because, when we have a negative experience like a mistake or failure or someone pointing out a flaw, we make the mistake of taking it personally. We have all taken things personally and have observed people in the process of taking things personally. What does it even mean to "take it personally"? I frame it with the concept of IVW. The negative event impacted the person's perceived value and worth. It wasn't simply a weakness or mistake that needed to be corrected; it became a reflection of their personal reputation and identity. Somehow, they decided that their value and worth decreased from that negative experience.

Our mental model produces to achieve both the micro and macro emotional goals as well as the assessment of our own value and worth. A present feeling is made up of both mood and emotion, evaluating the present probabilities of achieving our micro and macro emotional goals. *Our mood is an overall summation of our most recent successes and failures in moving closer to our ideal quality of life.*

When it comes to the overall evaluation of our value and worth, who has the authority and influence to add their opinions? There are many of us who are too concerned about what other people think, and there are many of us who don't care enough about what people think. The most mature among us absolutely care what others think while not letting it impact their value and worth as a person. Because the negative truth doesn't impact their value and worth, they are free to proactively seek out that information with the goal of eradicating the blind area and being better equipped in the growth process. Our ultimate goal is to have our subjective view of ourselves perfectly match the truth of how others see us and, more importantly, how God sees us (objective). See the chapter in my first book for the full explanation and process of IVW.

The final cause for our emotional storms is prior trauma. Like IVW, I took an entire chapter in my first book to cover trauma. Trauma can either be official, diagnosable trauma, which must be so significant that it threatens our long-term physical or emotional well-being, or it can simply be an emotionally intense experience that has long-term effects. As a professional, I completely understand diagnoses, but I try to help the client focus on the actual behaviors that need to change because of the human tendency to link a diagnosis to their value and worth. A diagnosis can be temporary, and therefore, should not define who we are. Even if a diagnosis is a permanent part of someone's DNA, e.g. a personality disorder or something biologically based like schizophrenia, it does not define their value or worth, nor is it their destiny. The same is true with the label of "trauma" because I have seen so many people do the same with that identity, which permanently decreases their value and worth. The difference is that while IVW is derived from within, trauma is derived from without, i.e. our environment or caused by other people. Our emotions get inflated because we experience a situation, and our mental model realizes this current situation is very similar to what happened before (the trauma). When that happens, our mental model acts like a backhoe, scoops a huge pile of emotion from the trauma, and dumps it right on this current situation.

The Third Tenet: All Negative Emotions are Exposing Something in Me

Now we get to the big one. All that negative emotion exposes something in me. At first blush, that sounds bad, but it is not. That's because it takes the power and authority over our emotions from the environment and gives it back to us. And much more powerfully, it is the doorway to the journey of our greatest growth. Let's imagine my wife does something that upsets me, which everyone who knows us knows my wife never has and never will do something to upset me. Whenever we argue, we aren't arguing but simply discussing one of Greg's shortcomings (just playing it safe, folks). But let's say, for instance, she does something that upsets me. What do I do? What do we all do? My first response is to start processing what my wife did or did not do that did not fulfill my expectations. "How dare she!" But I don't stop there, oh no. I start reflecting on how her mistake is related to some character flaw. I then start to really churn through the emotional energy by judging her motives. By now, I am really consumed, attacking her in my mind and heart, thinking of ways to get justice. More than that, I am forcing the solution to my emotions to squarely rest in her changing. Well now I am stuck because I have just concluded the solution to my negative emotion rests in something outside of my control.

That isn't to say that there is not something legitimate that I need to address with her. I am saying that the first step in this process is to discover what is being exposed to me. I must sift through all those interpretations and opinions my mental model produces, figure out which ones are true versus not, and ensure that all response paths pass the RHWR grid. After, I can then come to her with my rational point of frustration. If I just go to her with my first reactive, impulse response of emotions, it will involve significant emotional energy, and that is when I cause damage to her and our relationship and frankly, she doesn't deserve me to treat her like that. But don't worry, she's not helpless. After I do that, she is going to boomerang that emotional energy right back and educate me on how I psychologically blew it. All of that emotional energy that I so easily whipped up came from 1) my legitimate point of frustration, 2) several lies I may be believing about myself and her, 3) a need to defend myself because I may have allowed her offense to decrease my value and worth, or 4) that situation triggered a mental model memory from long ago where I felt vulnerable and exposed from some outside force more powerful than me.

Even if I successfully walk through this process, I need to figure out why my mental model produced that initial response in the first place. What "buttons" did she push? What insecurities did she expose in me? You can immediately see why we must first figure out what a situation is exposing in us before we can legitimately respond to any situation. I'm sure you can feel how hard this process can be because all these causes are nestled deep within us and have created a network of formulas that require recalibration. Finally, it may seem daunting to you because you have already suffered many consequences from these emotional storms. Take heart, that is exactly why I am writing this book. The Lord God above lends us His brilliance to help us be much more effective in our emotional management. The result is more confidence in our identity, value, and worth, and we become stronger than ever after being healed from the intense trauma we experienced. Now that the three tenets have been set, we move to the process of daily emotional management and unpack the emotions of insecurity, anxiety, fear, worry, anger and depression.

CHAPTER 4:

THE MATRIX OF INSECURITY

Set me as a seal upon your heart, as a seal upon your arm; for love is as strong as death, jealousy as cruel as the grave; its flames are flames of fire, a most vehement flame.

– Song of Songs 8:6

All negative emotions typically revolve around insecurity. I will define insecurity within the context of emotions as *something that is not firm or fixed, unsteady*. This is the gateway to the rest of the negative emotions as it relates to the foundation of our security, value, and worth. Insecurity may be the base or foundational level of other emotions in this book, but it is the richest as far as what it can reveal to us. Insecurity means we are not firmly founded in our identity. It is also related to the emotional intelligence skill of self-regard. Self-regard is the ability to respect and accept yourself—essentially liking the way you are.[5] We have an objective view of ourselves, our strengths and weaknesses, and we continue to work on ourselves. We accept where we are and are not trying to

---

[5] Stein, Steven J.; Book, Howard E.. The EQ Edge: Emotional Intelligence and Your Success (p. 68). Wiley. Kindle Edition.

hide our weaknesses or inflate our strengths. Insecurity would then be something we don't like about ourselves. But it doesn't end there since every person on Earth, ever, doesn't like some things about themselves. Well, except for those with certain personality disorders, which we won't get into here. The issue is not that we don't like something about ourselves; it is that we don't want anyone to point out or expose that thing. Like the blockbuster movies, the *Matrix* of insecurity describes the contrast between the experienced world and the real world. The experienced world is where all the focus and energy centers on the people who "made us" feel insecure. The real world is the unattractive world that shows us the real reason those comments have so much power.

Another foundational defining moment for me was when I was 14 years old and was working at the local hamburger joint in Schoolcraft, MI. I was the classic super sarcastic teenage guy, but all of us who worked there were friends and readily "talked trash" with each other. However, one time, I took it too far, and I teased this girl so badly that I made her cry. That's not the worst of it. As she was walking away, crying, I yelled out to her, "You wouldn't get so pissed off if it weren't true!" Don't judge me. That moment was an epiphany for me because I turned what I yelled to her on myself. I said, "Oh my gosh, Greg, every single time somebody cuts you down and you get defensive, get angry, and lash out, it's because it's true!" As with the other moments of revelation I mentioned, I started seeing that same truth apply to everyone. When people are either just teasing each other, or when they really are upset and want to insult one another and cut each other down, they choose to use information about that person that is negative and has truth to it. I have also observed situations when someone tried to insult another person, but the response by others was one of shock, saying, "What are you talking about? That person is nothing like that." Or we use another form of sarcasm and tease someone by saying something that obviously isn't true, and everybody laughs and agrees (because everyone knows it's not true). What I want to uncover is what's behind the true negative emotion of insecurity and how to respond to it.

There are three categories of insecurity. 1) It's true, but I don't want it exposed, 2) it's not true, but I believe it to be true, or 3) true or not true, someone is gossiping about me, and I'm insecure about what others are thinking and saying about me. If there is something I don't like about myself, whether it be a weakness, a failure, a physical feature, or my lack of success in any area, and someone points it out, what should I do? Well, if it's true, there's nothing to do but own it. Why hide it? Why get upset when someone points it out? It's true, so agree with it and say you agree that you wish it were different. Throughout the years, I developed a strong dislike of the times someone had power over me and my emotions. It took a long time, but I kept asking myself, "Why am I giving them this much power?" Instead of evaluating and processing them and attacking them in my mind, I started to figure out what it was exposing about me. The issue was in my emotional responses, not in other's choices. I don't want to give anyone, or anything in the environment, the ability to do something and then have me spend an incredible amount of time and energy responding to it, intrapersonal or interpersonally. Worse than this is when it's not true, but I believe it to be true. These normally come in broad-stroke insults like, "You're ugly, you're stupid, you're an idiot," etc. These insults are normally the insults that bullies use to gain power over another person. I have found the most effective response to these types of insults is to simply say, "Umm, okay." The only way for these insults to work would be for us to get angry and defensive, but we all know if we do that, it never achieves the desired emotional goals of peace and confidence because our negative response solidifies the lie in our mental models.

The last example deals with how to respond to gossip. Sadly, I developed this skill while I was a pastor. People gossip everywhere there is a community of people, including churches. There are always those people in our lives who don't like us and actively try to hurt us. One common way is to openly discuss those negative items about us, whether they are true or not. I recommend avoiding trying to control the gossiper. Of course, we should make every effort to build a relationship with those who think poorly of us, but sometimes that is not an achievable goal. Once I did everything I could to repair and develop that relationship, but to no avail (they kept gossiping), I then started to process what I was insecure about, namely the impact their gossip would have, so I turned my attention to those listening to the gossip. There are basically three groups of people that would hear this information: 1) those who love me, 2) those who don't know, or barely know me, or 3) those who somewhat know me, but they only have a limited exposure to me. I didn't even worry about those who loved me or those who didn't know me because those who loved me would either push back against the gossiper, ignore it, or come and tell me about it. Those who don't know me will just act confused and wait for the conversation with the gossiper to be over. The only group I concerned myself with were those who somewhat knew me. It was always a case-by-case example, but if I cared about what those people thought about me, I would proactively engage those people and simply own the truth. If it wasn't true, I'd ask them to have an open mind that what they heard may not be true about me. There are many other techniques to apply here, but the overall point is to not be afraid of what is true, own it, and if you can change it, work on it and go from there. Take the power away from the environment by having little to no negative emotion because you don't have any insecurities. Is it possible not to have any insecurities? The answer is yes. It is a great place to be. I have not perfected this in every situation, but I'm close, and even when I do blow it, it is easy to recover. Here are several **Mental Model Formula Formations** that we must adopt to *eradicate* insecurity from the list of negative emotions we experience.

If someone is "pushing your buttons," uninstall your buttons. Your buttons are your insecurities.

The issue isn't what they think of you; the issue is what you think of you. This formula summarizes the three kinds of insecurities above. The deeper issue is whether you **_need_** others to pursue you and validate you because your IVW is so weak that you need others to fill the vacuum.

Mental Model Formula Formation: Nothing bothers me unless it should. I encourage clients to repeat this phrase to themselves over and over. It is much more difficult to try and walk backward from a level of high emotional intensity, figuring out what is being exposed and then landing on the right amount of negative emotional energy.

The goal is to empower you and believe that your environment, whether it be your partner, your children, your employer, your extended family, or your church, has no power over you if you so choose. If your environment does expose a truth, then you need to have the right amount of negative emotions and own it, apologize for it, promise to work on it, etc. Negative emotions are healthy and valid if they are the right type and the right amount. If the criticisms are not valid, then nothing is being exposed, and if we all realize that if the criticism is not rational, healthy, wise, or right, *then it is exposing the criticizer, not the one being criticized.* I get frustrated with our current culture because it places the entire responsibility of managing our negative emotions on everyone but us. We are responsible for our actions, especially if they are not RHWR, but just because I am responsible for my actions, that does not make me culpable for your emotions, nor do your non-RHWR actions make you responsible for my emotions. I gladly and willingly free you from all burden, concern, or responsibility for my negative emotions!

What I'm teaching you is to train your mental model to *impulsively* go examine what is exposed, looking at everything and everyone in the environment, and passing blame and accusations out like a deck of cards. *Start* with "nothing bothers me," and then assess the entire situation through RHWR, and then land on the right amount of emotional energy. Remember the mental model process. Our formulas gather the information in each situation, interpret it, and then create a certain amount of emotional energy to proactively or reactively respond to the problem. Suppose our automatic assumption is that something needs adjusted in us first before something needs to be adjusted in us first before something needs to be fixed in our environment. In that case, we are going to live much more confident and peaceful lives.

CHAPTER 5:

LEAVE THE WINDOW OPEN FOR TINKERBELL

I sleep, but my heart is awake; it is the voice of my beloved! He knocks, saying, "Open for me, ... my love, my dove, my perfect one..." – Song of Songs 5:2

Now that I've laid the foundation, I turn to equipping you in your marriage. Question: If while sleeping tonight, Tinkerbell flew into your bedroom and sprinkled magical dust on you, and instead of the ability to fly, the magical dust perfected your marriage. When you woke up tomorrow, what would be different about *you*? I'm not asking what would be different with your marriage or what would be different about your spouse, but what would be different about you? One time, a couple came in for their first session, and when I asked that question, the wife leaned forward quickly to start talking, but when it registered in her mind what I was actually asking, she leaned back on the couch and didn't answer. I encouraged both to answer; it didn't matter who went first. After a few more awkward seconds, I said, "Isn't that funny? If I had asked what would be different about your marriage or what would be different about your spouse, each of you could probably talk for an hour. But when I ask what would be different about you, you're both speechless.

Therein lies the issue in this marriage." I call this question the first "pillar" because it needs to be immovable, tall, and always in focus. I want to set the same tone in marriage counseling as I do in individual counseling, i.e., successful counseling begins and ends with the client. I don't have the power to change anyone. Each spouse needs to pour all their emotional energy into evaluating and evolving themselves. However, I also alleviate their fears by assuring them that we will address every concern they have about their spouse.

Safety and Pursuit

Every relationship on Earth, ever, is about safety and pursuit. We all need to feel emotionally and relationally safe in our relationships, whether it be with our partner, our children, our family, our friends, our boss and co-workers, etc. Being safe is where we can bring in the grace and truth process stated earlier. We need to be safe when we expose our failures and weaknesses, and we need to be safe to speak the truth with one another. If we don't feel safe, the relationship will not go any deeper and richer, but the safer we feel to give and receive truth, the deeper and richer our relationships become. Although rhetorical, I ask each spouse, "Do you want your spouse to be safe with you in your heart?" They both say, "Of course!" I then ask them to remember and trust this whenever they don't feel safe with their spouse because they are arguing and are hurting. They both want the other person to feel safe, so when they don't feel safe, *that* is unnatural and an anomaly. I promise to equip them with all the communication skills they need to create a safe atmosphere in their marriage. As well, I ask them to remember the times in their relationship when they were at their best. The times when they were the most tender, the most in love, the most unselfish. The times when they would rest in each other's arms and say, "This is us." That is who they really are, and whenever they are angry and hurt, that is *not* who they truly are at their core, nor who they want to be. Now, being angry and hurt may absolutely be the norm in their relationship currently, but that is NOT who they are at their core. I want them to remember that as we start working on their marriage.

Now, this leads me to discuss pursuit. Outside of our spouses, pursuit is simply proactively seeking to spend time with one another to share our experiences and help one another improve our quality of life by sharing ideas, sharpening our minds in the deeper matters of life, and helping one another fulfill our destiny and leave a legacy for future generations. If someone doesn't feel safe, or we feel that we are pursuing others harder than they are pursuing us, the relationship will eventually end. With our boyfriends/girlfriends, fiancés, and spouses, pursuit includes the above, but more specifically, I define pursuit as *a specific <u>romantic</u> action we do to create a positive emotional experience in our partners.*

With that definition, I ask the husband first to ask his wife, "Do you feel like I'm currently pursuing your heart?" The answers are either in the negative or positive, with the occasional "Sometimes." If positive or sometimes, I then have him ask the follow-up question, "Am I blowing you away in how hard I'm pursuing you?" That answer is almost always, "No." The wife isn't off the hook because I have her ask the same questions, and the answers are almost always the same. I encourage them and reassure them that it is okay because that is why they are here and that I promise to equip them in this area as well. The second "pillar" is set right next to the principle of pursuit. I call it the *brag about* question. Just as the first pillar is focused on each person burning their emotional energy evaluating what would be different about them, this pillar focuses on doing just that under the topic of pursuit. Instead of asking their spouse if they feel pursued, they can get the same answer by asking themselves, "Is my spouse compelled, motivated, or excited to brag about how incredible of a spouse I am? Would they say of me, 'I have never been loved like this before, and I can't imagine being loved like this by anyone else!'" If the answer to that question is "no", *it is illegal for me to have one complaint about my spouse until I get them to that point*. Both pillars are there to be immovable, never out-of-sight reminders of the original vows we made at the altar: that our promise was to create an atmosphere of safety and pursuit for our spouse. Further, the goal is not just to create this atmosphere; our goal is actually to *maximize* pursuit and *maximize* safety.

If the couple is Christian, then they understand that God created marriage, and his goal for marriage is to emulate the type of safety the Trinity shares with one another. Each member of the Trinity experiences being known by the other member; there is complete safety and a full understanding and appreciation for their role, as well as the roles of the other members of the Trinity. I will spend time later in this book discussing the unique roles husbands and wives have within the marriage. As we all know, our culture has worked hard to disparage these roles, but I truly believe that the pendulum has swung so far away from a biblical marriage that many in our culture, even if not Christian, are starting to see how ridiculous and foolish our culture has become. The culture has shifted so far away from the Christian paradigm, and we are in the worst state we have ever been. Many are tired of the foolishness and choosing to go back to what God has prescribed for marriage thankfully. Secondly, God wants us to maximize our pursuit of one another, and he has shown us what it can be like in the relationship between King Solomon and his wife in the book of the Bible, Song of Songs. The way they are absolutely infatuated with one another is what many of us have experienced at the height of our relationship with our spouses, which was most likely during our engagement, wedding, and honeymoon. The way a couple shares their vows with letters and poems is similar to the Song of Songs. It is magical and beautiful. Most couples go through the same process. They meet, the woman blushes, the guy gives a really awkward smile and starts emulating Thumper from the movie *Bambi,* and they start dating. Their relationship blossoms to the point of engagement and marriage, and then the beautiful, romantic aura just seems to dissipate. Why? I believe that the couple naturally goes into *roommate* and *business partner* mode and start working together to build the foundation and financial stability of their lives, which is exactly what should happen. But they forget to work just as hard to keep the mindset they had while they were dating and engaged. Think of that mindset. They were the most gracious, flexible, and consumed with the experience of the other person during that time. Allow me to give a stark warning to anyone who is in a dating relationship or engaged: if what I just described is foreign to you and your partner does not have that mindset, dump them faster than your murder weapon after your crime. I know, horrible analogy, but you get the urgency, right? However, considering the pillars I described, you may first want to evaluate if you have that mindset yourself. When we hear from old married couples that marriage is hard work. It's not because we have to work hard arguing with one another to come to a resolution. What it means is that keeping that gracious, flexible, and captivated mindset fresh and alive throughout our marriage is hard work, but it's worth it.

-10 to +10

Next, to get their view of the overall temperature of the relationship, I'll ask my clients to rate their marriage currently according to a number line, from -10 to +10. A -10 would represent them on the verge of separation or divorce, 0 would be there isn't anything bad in the relationship, and nothing really powerful either (they are like roommates), and +10 would be like the movie *The Notebook*. I am still surprised that regardless of the couple's age, everyone seems to know that reference even though they never saw the movie. However, I also describe +10 as being a state of relationship where they both would say, "I literally don't know how our relationship can be any better." I also feel compelled to say that +10 is not perfection, and that a +10 relationship *is* possible. Before they rate the marriage, I explain one more thing about the number line. The distance from -10 to +5 is shorter than the distance from +6 to +10. I want the couple to understand that that range is a special zone. It is where you both feel your spouse "blows you away" sometimes in their pursuit of you. I have a mindset of "I have no rights" and "whatever she wants, she gets," and it is a place where we naturally try to out-serve one another. We are always asking if we can do something for the other person and where we will surprise one another by doing one another's chores (including our own). I tell couples to see their anniversary as their next wedding date. We need to have the mindset that every year, we need to win our spouse back to the altar. Think about how that changes our perspective. This zone has a completely different feel to it, and I won't lie to you, it is hard to get into this zone.

I explain that between +5 and +6, there is a reef like the reef in the movie *Castaway*. In that movie, Tom Hanks plays a FedEx pilot who is the lone survivor of his plane crash. He is stranded on an island, and even after successfully constructing a raft, he is unable to go out to sea because at a certain distance from shore, a barrier reef creates waves that keep thrusting his raft back toward shore. It is only after he constructs a makeshift sail that uses the wind to give him that final thrust over the reef into the open waters. The gap between +5 and +6 is like that reef. I have worked with couples that experience an overall positive marriage (+1 to +5), but there is still a feeling of "it could be so much better." Once we overcome our own reef, we are finally in the "zone" where we constantly look for ways to be unselfish. It is a sweet, sweet place to be. I truly believe with all my heart that every one of us not only wants to experience that zone, but we truly want to *give* that experience to our spouse. However, because of our world, many of us have been hurt in relationships and become jaded, so we lower our expectations and, at best, are content to hover around a +3 in our relationships, which means that is also how much effort we put into the relationship. Take courage, and I will equip you with the skills to overcome that relational reef. But you must create the sail driven by the winds of commitment and motivation to thrust your marriage over it.

After I explain that zone, I always ask the husband first rate the state of their marriage. The husband is the thermostat for the relationship, while the wife is the thermometer. He tries to set the temperature for the relationship, but it is the wife who reflects the true temperature of the relationship! Whatever his rating, I am more concerned that when the wife reveals her score, they are relatively close to one another, even if the rating is closer to -10. There have been two times over my 30 years of working with couples where there was an astonishing gap between the husband's rating and the wife's rating. What is even funnier is that both couples had the exact same rating! The husband rated the marriage at a +5, and the wife rated the marriage -7. Oh boy. Bless his heart. By the way, guess which partner consistently rates the marriage higher? You guessed it, the man. It doesn't matter where the couple rates the marriage because I have a high success rate with couples, even if they are close to -10. I just need to know where they are emotionally before we get into why. One more point I want to make. I would much rather see a great deal of negative emotion expressed over apathy. When the couple is still experiencing anger, it tells me they are still emotionally invested in the relationship. Anger is always a result of hurt and fear, and they are using anger to correct the problems. If either spouse is apathetic, then I am concerned because the energy needed to make those corrections is absent. Apathy is the exact opposite of empathy. Both words come from the Greek word *pathos,* which means suffering. Em-pathos means to suffer with, a-pathos means there is no suffering, no passion, no emotion.

Three Phases of Marriage Counseling

About 99% of couples reach out to me and state communication as not only one of the key topics they want help with but the main reason that motivates them to seek help. I tell couples that the first phase in marriage counseling is to *not cause further damage.* Every couple has legitimate topics they need to discuss, but the problem is when they discuss these topics, they argue, start insulting each other's character, maturity, emotionality, and motives, and then cause damage to the relationship. Now, they require more discussions to recover from the hurt they caused before they can get back to discussing the original issue. In the next chapter, I will provide several communication skills and how to use them. A note to other counselors: several couples come to me because their last therapist made several errors that I don't understand, but they are common enough that I feel the need to address them. First, they would never say this, but by the way they practice they only practice "empathy" therapy, or just talk-and-listen therapy because their goal is simply for the client to feel comfortable instead of actually providing skills, techniques, and solutions. The therapist models what good listening looks like by paraphrasing what each person is saying, which is great, but great listening alone doesn't help couples solve problems. Second, if the therapist helps the couple solve problems, they don't equip the couple with the knowledge to be fully independent and autonomous in communication and problem-solving to be successful outside of the counseling session. Finally, each of us have to work extra hard to build rapport and show lack of bias with the opposite gender spouse. In the first session, I joke with the husband, telling him that I am going to be 10 times harder on him than his wife. I assume that she will assume, because I'm a male therapist, that I'm going to automatically take the man's side. Joking aside, I do work hard at making sure each spouse feels heard and understood by me. The worst-case scenario is when the therapist can't help themselves and is obviously bringing their own bias and experience into the session. Counselors, we can't impart what we don't possess. While we all have rough seasons in marriage, if you can't honestly say that the couple you are counseling can model their marriage after yours, then you shouldn't do marriage counseling. If you are single, then you can certainly do marriage counseling, but if you are single and still wounded from past relationships, then you shouldn't be counseling couples either. Again, every marriage has growth areas, but the key litmus test is whether the couple you are counseling could model their marriage after your marriage (if they knew you personally, of course). We know the same is true ethically concerning seeing individual clients and ensuring your success in thoughts, emotions, and relationships are greater than that of the individual with whom you're working. Please ensure you can equip each couple with all the skills they need to be successful in their marriage.

The second phase of marriage counseling introduces the system of *scheduling the minimum*. There is much to unpack here, which

I'll get to later, but first, I will give the history of this technique. Early in my career, when I was just beginning to work with couples, a very common issue would come up, the love language of quality time. As I stated earlier, many women have quality time as one of their love languages. In session, the wife would say she wanted more (quality) time with her husband. As you might expect, the husband would try and convince her they spend plenty of time together, to which the wife would lay down the "quality" card, to which the husband would just look at her cross-eyed because he had no idea what that even meant. However, I also noticed another common theme that would present itself. Some women never felt fulfilled in this love language when, after diving deeper into both the quality and quantity of time the couple actually spent together, she should have been. After seeing this pattern, it became clear that it was all a matter of subjectivity based on preconceived expectations. There are wives who spend less quality time with their husbands and are content and fulfilled, while other wives who had more quality time with their husbands, were emotionally feeling like their husbands basically ignored them.

The common cycle I noticed was when wife proposed more quality time, the husband either tried to present evidence that they were spending enough time together or got defensive and complained about everything he had to do, feeling like a failure (emotional goal of significance being blocked) that he couldn't get it all done and didn't feel successful in any area of his life. His dismissal of her request would make his wife feel as if he didn't want to spend more time with her, leaving her to feel unimportant to him. His anger would make her feel relationally and emotionally unsafe (emotional goal of security being blocked). What a mess! At this point, I would pull them out of this micro topic to a macro view of our common struggles. Our life is like a pie. The pie is only so big because we only have so much time to work with. Each slice of the pie represents an area of our life that needs our time and attention. Time with our spouse, time with our children, time with the Lord, time for work and chores, time for exercise, time for downtime and recreation, and time for growth and development. The problem is that each of these areas falls under the banner of "the more, the better." The more time we spend in each of these areas, the better it would be, but that is entirely impractical because time is a limited resource. We need to frame each area as a goal. How will we know when we are subjective in each area? It is subjective, sure, but we must try and make it objective and adjust expectations accordingly.

Once we define what success looks like in each area, then schedule the *minimum* amount of time it would take to achieve success there. Begin with the areas that always seem to lose the priority battle, like time with the Lord and mediation and/or time to exercise. Ask yourself what is the minimum amount of time you need each day/week to achieve the goal? For prayer and meditation, would 30 minutes a day achieve your goal of having a close relationship with the Lord? What is the minimum amount of time to achieve the goal of being healthy? Schedule it . . . literally. Put all the areas of the pie on your calendar. This ensures that all your values that fall under the macro emotional goal of your highest quality of life are achieved.

What about recovery time? This is time to refill our emotional tanks. Emotional energy is a limited resource like time and money; we only have so much of it, it's limited. I have worked with clients that are on opposite ends of the spectrum. Some clients desperately need downtime, but when they sit down to turn their brain off and watch a movie, they feel guilty because they feel they should work more, do more around the house, exercise, etc. The technique/system of scheduling the minimum frees them from this irrational guilt because they can remind themselves that they are accomplishing all the goals of their live value pie of their life values/goals (time for relationships, exercise, etc.). I also have clients at the other end of the spectrum who spend way too much time on their phones, playing video games, or watching TV. Scheduling the minimum amount of time in the very area of their life that they say they value also forces them to evaluate and ask themselves, "How much recovery time do I really need daily or weekly?" Once they schedule the minimum in every area of their life, they can be free to play video games and not worry about frustrating their spouse because over the amount of time spent in that area. Think about this truth in marriages:

We often attack the thing we see as an obstacle to our goal. As you might imagine, I cannot tell you the number of times I have heard wives complain to their husbands about the amount of time they spend on video games. The husbands defend themselves and say that it's not wrong to play video games, they work hard and need time to relax. Some even defend playing video games by declaring the age-old adolescent defense of playing video games develops hand-eye coordination and strategic thinking. First, husbands and wives, it's not about the video games (or the golf, or sports on TV), it's about the belief the wife has that her husband is not achieving all the goals of his life value pie. Second, husbands/boyfriends, schedule the minimum in all of areas, and evaluate how much time you need to refill your emotional tank. Once you determine it, schedule it! Finally, husbands/boyfriends, of all the ways to spend your time, is the path of video games the most RHWR way to achieve the goal of emotional recovery time? If you really wanted to achieve hand-eye coordination, I'm sure you did that about a decade ago. Is playing video games the most effective way to do it? Seriously? How about playing a musical instrument? Nevertheless, it's not about the video games, of course you are free to play them, and it's okay!(is this sentence necessary- it's a repeat) There are five key elements of scheduling the minimum with our spouses, and I will address this later. (this sentence doesn't give closure to paragraph nor idea presented- not needed)

The third phase of marriage counseling is to equip the couple with the skills of the +6 to +10 area of the number line. This is the culmination of the two pillars. Mastering this phase moves the pillars from in front of us to below us, from unfamiliar concepts to the very foundation of our marriage, from an idea outside of us to becoming the decorative cornerstones in the home of the heart of our marriage. When we practice these principles, we come to realize this is what we wanted to experience when we fell in love with our spouses. I discussed this in my first book, however my first marriage ended after 19 ½ years of marriage. Believe it or not, we filed for divorce on our 19th wedding anniversary. Even though I was in the ministry and a counselor, the core of our marriage was deteriorating. We never really fought, we respected one another greatly in ministry, and we were also very united and solid in our parenting. Unfortunately, the negative emotions in our hearts were never dealt with, and eventually, took their toll. I had an emotional affair and our marriage never recovered. The worst day of my life, without question, was the day we told our three beautiful teenagers we were getting a divorce. The pain was so intense and so deep that I shudder every time I think about it. I wish we would have "blown up" the issues in our marriage and dealt with them. We tried counseling, but it was surface at best. We hardly ever fought, but looking, back I wish we would have had some knock-down, drag-out fights because maybe that would have forced us to deal with the wounds. Earlier, when I was harsh on my fellow counselors by saying if their marriage could not be a model for the couples, they are counseling or they should not be coaching couples, I was sharing my testimony, not my opinion. I remarried an absolutely incredible woman who is beautiful inside and out. If you met her, you would agree. Everyone loves my wife, Lisa. She is proof of the grace of God in my life. Early in our relationship, she pursued and loved my children, and I believe part of their own healing from our divorce can be credited to my wife Lisa. Further, the entirety of my first book is the product of the hard healing work I did for years after my divorce. I tell clients that everything in my counseling philosophy ran through the heart and soul of Greg, and they are receiving the fruit of that work. I can say I am healed, at peace, and am stronger now than I have ever been. I wouldn't wish what I went through on anyone, but I am stronger now than I have ever been. Thanks to the absolute grace of God, I've been able to heal my relationship with my ex-wife and even her family. I love them and miss them. Praise God for what he has done. Our marriage can absolutely be a model for every couple that I counsel. We live in the +6 to +10 zone of the number line, and let me tell you, it is a sweet, sweet place to be.

CHAPTER 6:

STOP CAUSING FURTHER DAMAGE

I am my beloved's, and his desire is towards me. – Song of Songs 7:10

In this chapter, I will give several communication and problem-solving skills. I promise to equip you with all the skills you need to be effective in your communication with your partner or spouse. Other than devastating actions like affairs, substance abuse, or emotional/verbal/physical abuse, poor communication skills are the main cause of thrusting a marriage into the negative side of the number line. I ask couples for a three-way verbal covenant that they will promise to practice these skills. They need to get these skills into their mental models so their mental models will automatically suggest these skills in the future instead of what their mental models suggest to them now, hence the poor communication! Not only that, I ask that couples use the exact working of these skills, not that there is any power in the words of the skills themselves, but when you use the actual words of the skills, it "interrupts" the emotional pattern of the couple's arguments. These key words are foreign to their mental models, so the energy shifts from the emotional center to the frontal lobe, where thinking happens. We need these skills the most during times of emotional highpoints when it is hard to turn off the auto-pilot poor responses. During times of tension, specifically requesting the use of a certain skill can "shock the system" and help break the pattern. Know this, it takes a long time for couples to implement these skills, so be prepared for failure. At the beginning of each session, I ask, "Since we last met, were there any opportunities to use the skills, and how did it go?" The first thing I see improve with clients is the time it takes for them to recover from an argument begins to shorten. After the argument, they start to see themselves more objectively and say, "Crap, we did it again!" Slowly but surely, there is a downward trend to the process. Fights start decreasing in intensity. From a "10" to a "9" to an "8" and so on. Second, the duration of the argument and the calming of emotions decreases. Third, the frequency of their arguments *decrease* because they've become more skilled and start to implement the relational building processes such as pursuit and scheduling the minimum. The first set of skills helps to recover from the hurt caused in by the argument. The second set helps to not escalate to the point of causing damage, and the third set of skills helps in developing richer communication and problem-solving skills.

How to Recover from the Hurt We Caused

5-Minute Retract
This is used the day after a bad argument where the couple had a bad fight and exchanged some very hurtful words. Examples are, "I wish I would have never married you!" or "You are such a _____!" What I have found is that there may be 10-15 hurtful things said,

but there are only two or three things that still "stick" like an arrow in the side. Even though we know what they said to us is either not true or we know they didn't truly mean it, I have found that it still will hurt days, weeks, even years later. Proverbs 18:21 says, "Death and life *are* in the power of the tongue, and those who love it will eat its fruit."[6] As we speak death to our partner, we must pull out those arrows and speak life (encouragement) into our spouse's heart. Following the "ladies first" principle, let her go first. She simply says, "Would you please retract when you said (or when you called me) ..." The man's reply is simply, "Yes. I absolutely retract that. I didn't mean it and wish I wouldn't have said it. Will you please forgive me?" Make sure you ask the question at the end and receive the answer "yes." The man follows the same pattern and they take turns until both can't think of anything else. Think of it as if you are withdrawing the arrows not only from your most recent fight, but every arrow from the very beginning of the relationship.

One word of warning: sometimes spouses will deny they ever spoke that "arrow." A common theme throughout these communication techniques is to argue over the details of past events. There is no way to prove what was/was not spoken, how we did or did not come across, or what we did or didn't do. This is the most fruitless and exhausting argument couples have. "You weren't wearing a blue shirt; it was a pink shirt!" Who cares, and how are you going to prove it? More than that, do you *really* think your spouse is going to suddenly agree with you? Quit trying to prove the past! In this technique, simply reply to the same way.

---

[6] The Holy Bible, New King James Version, Copyright © 1982 Thomas Nelson

The issue is not whether you actually said i;, the issue is that your partner thinks you did and feels as if an arrow remains in their heart from it. I am glad they are asking me to pull it out, *especially* if I don't believe I said it; I want that arrow out either way!

Instant Validation

This is another technique to use after a bad argument. When we are confronted by our partner for the hurt we caused, we often get defensive, and our spouse starts to escalate again because we won't own it. A common thing we all do is say, "The only reason I did that is because you...." This means we are literally trying to validate our poor response because they did something wrong. Does that ever work? Or more importantly, does it pass the RHWR grid? Of course not. To keep this from happening, simply say "You are absolutely right in that.... I have no argument or defense against that; what you are saying is absolutely true. I own it." A powerful instant validation I give to Christian couples is to take turns saying to one another, "Regardless of what you did or said, Jesus would *never* have responded to you the way I did when I _____." Take turns owning the fact that you should have never responded that way.

Preventing the Escalation

Are we safe?

If you have a concern and want to ask a legitimate question or make a statement, but are concerned it will trigger your partner, simply ask "Are we safe right now?" If your spouse asks you that question, commit to thinking, *"My partner has thought through this and believes the concern is legitimate but is fearful I'll respond poorly."* Simply respond with, "Yes" or even better, "Of course we are pooky snooks! Ask away!" Now to be sure, when that question is asked in the future, you will pause, swallow hard, and start to sweat. The question is a short-answer question, like "did you . . . like you said you would?" or a short, quick correction like, "When you commit us to doing something without running it by me, it's frustrating." The spouse either simply answers the question or responds with an instant validation. Please don't ask if you're safe and then drop a bomb like, "Why don't you love me?!!!" That type of question is loaded and there is another technique for that type of question. Another way to use this technique is if a normal conversation starts to escalate, either of you can simply say, "We are safe right now. We don't need to be afraid, or defensive, or insecure." Hopefully, you both will pause and lower the cannons of your defensiveness.

Are we good?

This technique can be used by either, but it is most often used by the guy. My wife and I have used this technique hundreds of times, and it works wonders. When you aren't currently discussing anything, doing stuff around the house and hanging out, and you sense from your spouse through their non-verbal presence, and there is a "feeling in the air" that your partner is upset about something. If you're wondering if it's you, simply ask, "Are we good?" 99% of the time it will be, "Yeah, we are good! I'm just thinking about something." If we never ask, we might over think it and even get an attitude, get defensive in our minds, start insulting our spouses in our minds, and begin a silent feud that can ignite with the smallest communication. It's amazing how immature we can be sometimes. I say husbands use this more is because most husbands live and die by "happy wife, happy life," but take it too far and find themselves just trying to appease their wives by trying to avoid getting corrected by them. Some guys have tried to do a form of this technique and ask, "Are you mad at me?" or "What's your problem?" and my favorite one said by a husband, "Are you in a mood?" Even if the husband is trying to be "in tune" with his wife, these questions are not received this way. As well, if his wife was good with him before, she may feel frustrated because his question just annoyed her. When we receive this question, it can also help us become more self-aware on what we are communicating non-verbally. The question, "Are we good?" can also mean, "Are you okay?" If you answer positively, then be self-aware that your countenance may need to be adjusted. I strongly, strongly advise that if you were the one who asked, "Are we good?" that you don't follow up with suggesting they tell that to their face. Bad juju!

Instant Clarification

I could almost write an entire book on this one technique. The truth is that 99% of all arguments start with a misunderstanding. The misunderstanding most often comes from our non-verbal communication or how we "came across" to one another. The misunderstanding can also come from our verbal communication, or our choice of words. Most people are simply not masters of using the exact words that most closely align with what they are trying to say. As a matter of fact, some of my clients' word choices make me want to say, "Could you have said that any *worse* than what you just said?" Sometimes it's just hilarious some of the things I have heard come out of a person's mouth when they are trying to express themselves, it's a train wreck.

This technique is the one that absolutely needs to be used the most by couples *but is the hardest to use*. Why? Because the very moment it needs to be used is when you feel your internal "furnace kick on" and your defenses bolt up. You become offended and angry because your spouse communicated (verbally or non-verbally) something insulting, derogatory, offensive, or critical. At this very moment, the most glorious thing that could happen is for you to remember what I said earlier about both of you wanting your partner to be safe and that you both want to experience one another at your best. Nevertheless, that is just a dream early on in marriage counseling and will never happen, but take heart, in time, your mental model will produce those truths instead of offense.

When we get triggered, say, "This is how I am receiving you right now; you are saying that I am _____." Your partner simply responds with, "If I'm coming across that way, I don't mean to, I'm sorry. Let me replace that with what I'm really trying to communicate." If used this way, you will be amazed at how successful the conversation flows. It halts the offense and allows the misunderstanding to clear up so it doesn't escalate any further. But nevertheless, it is just a nice dream at this point. I have found that it becomes too hard for the one whose furnace kicked on to say, "This is how I am receiving you . . ." The furnace normally produces the reply that confronts the person on how they came across. If the words "came across" are not used, the response will be the part that comes after "This is how I am receiving you . . ." Here are some examples, so just add either "You are coming across as . . ." or "This is how I'm receiving you . . ." at the beginning of each of these.

"You think you are so perfect!"

"Don't treat me like I'm stupid."

"You think I just sit on my a** all day and do nothing."

"You think you are such a better parent than me."

There are obviously a million more, but you get the idea. If the prefix phrase of, "You're coming across . . ." is used, the immediate response is denial, "No I'm not," or "That's not what I said," or "That is not what I meant." The first two are completely ineffective considering what I pointed out earlier about trying to prove the past. There is no solution to he said/she said, he did/she did or come across arguments. It's impossible to prove, but even though you agree with me right now, along with every other couple I have ever worked with, we just can't help ourselves. It's not that we are really trying to prove what we did or didn't say or do, I believe the reason why we get triggered and engage again (for the millionth time) in this fruitless argument is because we are trying to prove that our partner is lying, wrong, clueless, or stupid. Of course, that never gets proven, and your partner then gets offended that you are attacking their character. Then, the battle for moral superiority commences, and at the end of the day, you both win the award for biggest loser of the argument. Of the responses above, the one that sometimes works is, "That is not what I meant," but the first thing your partner thinks or says is, "But that is how you came across." If you say, "That is not what I meant," then you need to replace it with what you did mean and simply say that you didn't mean to come across that way. It is very common for the spouse who was triggered to forget to use the first half of this technique. If your partner fails to use the first half of this technique, then you know you need to use the second half of the technique when you hear some form of "you" followed by an accusation of something absolutely shocking because they are accusing you of saying something, thinking something, or coming across in a certain way that is a mile away from what you meant and you are shocked they are accusing you of this. If that happens, then just use the second half of this technique, "If I came across that way, I'm sorry, I did not mean to. Let me replace it with what I want to communicate." Then, say what you wanted your partner to receive the first time around. This can be used with accusations of what we said. We could reply with, "If I said that, I agree with you, that was completely wrong. Let me say what I wanted you to hear." It is easier for the partner being accused of the offense to use the second part of Instant Clarification because their furnaces are likely not kicked on at this point. I always say it is the responsibility of the person who is offended because chances are high that your partner is not aware of the way in which they were received and is simply talking.

Let me now go deeper and discuss the emotionality of these communication exchanges. A well-known paradigm of this is called the Parent-Adult-Child model. The goal is to always stay in an adult-to-adult mode. I use three T's to describe the adult-to-adult exchange, which are Tame, Teachable, and Truthful. In a healthy and mature adult conversation, we are *tame*; we are calm, cool, and collected. Second, we are *teachable* and open to being corrected and interested in what the other person knows that we may not be thinking. We are open to their way of thinking. Finally, we are also willing to speak *truthfully* to one another (in love) when we need to. That is the way it is supposed to work. When a couple is in adult-to-adult mode, things are great, but what often happens is one of the partners shifts into parent mode. Parent mode is "corrective" mode, either verbally or non-verbally. But please note: one partner shifting into the parent mode is not always their fault. That partner may be fully exercising all three T's, but when they speak the truth, even if done in love, the partner on the receiving end shifts themselves down into the child mode, which is described as offended and defensive. Thus, the one partner has *received* their partner as being too corrective and shifting their partner up into parent mode without the other partner even knowing it.

Since no one wants to feel corrected and attacked, the partner quickly morphs into the parent role to reclaim their dignity and set their partner straight. This is when we would say something completely unrelated and defensive like, "My mother? What about your mother?" for example, even though you are talking about something completely different. Their partner then shifts down into the child role and becomes defensive, and then, for the same reasons, thrusts themselves into the parent mode, but this time it's intentional. The rest of the conversation then goes from adult-to-adult to parent-child-parent child. At that point the couple has reached the point of no return (great album by Kansas) and will need to practice the recovery techniques discussed above. Both should have stayed in the adult role, and even if their partner shifts and goes between child and parent roles, they can remain in the adult role by staying calm and using the technique of Instant Clarification. If they both blow it and take turns shifting into the child-parent roles, one of them will need to come to their senses and revive the conversation using the techniques outlined in this chapter. If they hold fast and stay there, their partner will eventually slow down and come back to the adult role themselves. I liken this exchange to the desktop toy people have in their offices with the metal balls that continue to go back and forth using kinetic energy. What happens if you stop one of those metal balls? The ball on the other side has no choice but to stop because there isn't any more kinetic energy to keep the movement happening. Once one partner stays in the adult role, the kinetic energy of defensiveness and correction is drained from the conversation.

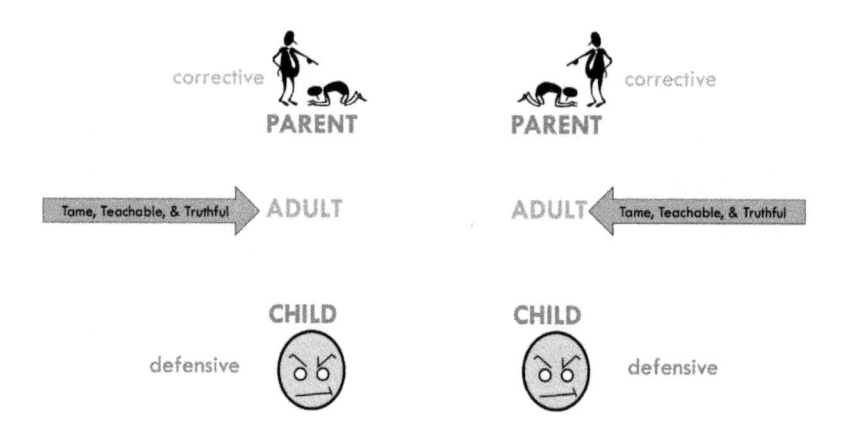

corrective **PARENT**	**PARENT** corrective
Tame, Teachable, & Truthful → **ADULT**	**ADULT** ← Tame, Teachable, & Truthful
defensive **CHILD**	**CHILD** defensive

Instant Clarification and the paradigm of adult-parent-child is where the third tenet of *all negative emotion is exposing something in you* applies. While these techniques are good, it would be more effective to figure out why our spouse would have to use the technique, "Are we safe?" to begin with. Why is your spouse concerned about you getting triggered in the first place? If you know they are right in their criticism of you, you should own it without any emotion. Who cares how your spouse comes across to you? The fact that your furnace kicks on is your issue, not theirs. Uninstall your buttons. If you believe your spouse is criticizing you, then why don't you first use the principles in the chapter on insecurity? Is what they are saying true? Own it. If their criticism not true, then why get so upset? The issue isn't what your partner thinks of you, the issue is what you think of you. Master the mental model formula formation of *nothing bothers me unless it should*. If your spouse does come across a certain way, or you perceive them shifting into parent mode, you *should* address it and use the techniques, in a tame way. If you find your emotional state hijacks your ability to stay the adult, then you need to figure out what is being exposed in you. You may be able to use the techniques I provide in my first I^3 book to process the negative emotions of insecurity, anxiety, fear, worry, anger, and depression, but if you consistently experience your emotional energy getting inflated and you know you are always way more emotional about any particular topic than you should be, then you need to do work on your identity, value, and worth or go through the process of healing from any trauma you experienced. You need to first do the intrapersonal (internal) work first and then use the interpersonal techniques to help you, and your partner walk through any topic that needs work. Both of you may need to put this book down and go to my first I[3] book and walk into your negative emotions. This is only way you will find the powerful intimacy found in the level of safety of the Trinity and the level of pursuit of the Song of Songs.

RHWR
RHWR can also be used as a communication technique to keep ourselves from escalating. RHWR is an objective truth that hovers above us all. In communication, we are all *accountable* to it, but we can also *appeal* to it. When communicating, we should hold ourselves accountable in real time by assessing our thoughts and words. We often make black-and-white statements using always and never, or we accuse our spouse of having wrong motives, or we just attack them unjustly. If something slips out that does not pass the RHWR test, then we can own it by saying, "I'm sorry, that was not rational," and then correct it. As well, instead of getting defensive, we can appeal to RHWR by responding to our partner and say something like, "Listen, that is not healthy." Instead of dismissing you, the partner is now forced to prove that what they did or said *was* healthy.

The Process of Addressing Unfulfilled Expectations
Negative emotions are produced when our expectations are not fulfilled. If our expectations are fulfilled, we don't have any emotions, and if our expectations are exceeded, we have positive emotions. If we are applying the mindset of *nothing bothers me unless it should*, this is a process we can use to figure out if we

should have negative emotions. So how much should something bother us? What is the true, realized negative impact of your partner's "offense"? What is the most effective and RHWR response to that offense and how much emotional energy do you need to do that action? The evaluation of emotional energy should match the weight of importance of the topic itself. I give couples what I call the *spectrum of importance*. This is a spectrum where we place topics under the appropriate category of importance and meaning to us. It is subjective in that *we* determine how important things are to us, but it is also objective in that we challenge ourselves in that placement. There are some things that should be more important to us than it is and vice versa. Additionally, we need to consider our partner's own spectrum and placement of topics in order to be aligned in how we make decisions and respond to topics. On the lower end of importance are *opinions* (neutral, no real importance either way, such as the color of paint to use in a room), *preferences* (I prefer Chinese over Mexican tonight), *wants/desires* (I really want to no go anywhere this weekend), and on the higher end of importance are *values* (parenting goals, for example), *convictions* (I'm not okay with either of us using marijuana), and *laws or dealbreakers* (infidelity, abuse, or not practicing the same faith). When working through any problem with your spouse, you need to decide how important it is for the two of you to agree. As you might imagine, we can misattribute the weight of each topic, giving more weight to "lower tier" topics. Another way to say it is we *moralize preferences, wants, and desires*, by getting extremely offended and hurt over something that is not that important. Don't put that level of weight on items that ultimately don't matter. When you do, you dump a lot of negative emotional energy on your spouse that they don't deserve and cause damage to the relationship. So why would we do that? It doesn't make sense, right?

The Meaning Behind the Topic

When our spouse comes off too intense about a topic that is only an opinion, preference, or want/desire, it is not necessarily about the topic itself, it is about a deeper meaning behind it. For example, when making decisions about finances, the calendar, or even where to go out to eat, the current discussion reminds the partner of a deeper issue in the relationship. It could be that the partner feels that you always have the final say of these items and that you never defer to their preference. Perhaps they feel you are constantly overruling them, even without intention. This is where we address *intent vs. impact*. We so often excuse ourselves with the statement, "I didn't mean to!" Okay, great, but that doesn't nullify the impact you are having on others. If your spouse is feeling a certain way that could be described using "always" or "never," please don't make the mistake of correcting them (I know many marriage books advise against using these words, which is true, but why not overlook the word and go to the meaning behind it instead of being a nerd and correcting the accuracy of the word itself?). When our partner is too upset about the topic under discussion, then exercise your emotional intelligence and realize it's not about the topic, but about what the topic is representing. Ask your partner, "What is it about this topic that is so upsetting to them? What is it about the current topic that keeps reminding them of something they have brought up several times before?" When you ask that, you will get to the real issue. On the other hand, if there isn't any deeper meaning behind it and the intensity is too high, then both partners can decrease the intensity by simply acknowledging where on spectrum the topic fits, realizing it's not that big of a deal.

An Illustration from Couple's Who Decide to Live Together

When I am working with a young couple and they tell me they made the decision to move in together, I ask them why they don't just get married? They either downplay the "piece of paper," saying they don't need a piece of paper to be committed to one another. I ask them if they really believe the only difference is the piece of paper? The more common explanation is they want to see if they are compatible with one another. I then teach them the spectrum of importance and ask them if they have had enough deeper talks to see if they align on the deeper issues of their values, convictions, laws, philosophy, beliefs, etc. They always say they have and feel they are aligned well. If that is the case, then my question is, "What do you think you will discover living together that would be a dealbreaker for the relationship, especially if you already are aligned on the weightier topics?" The only things left for them to discover when it comes to compatibility is the normal roommate stuff. I tell them that if they end their relationship after moving in together, it will be because 1) they change their minds on the weightier items or act against them (cheating), 2) they damage safety and quit pursuing to the point of dissolving the relationship, or 3) if neither of those happen, then the only thing that will end the relationship will be their selfishness and immaturity. If you ask your partner to do or not do something over and over, and the request is RHWR, and they aren't changing, then walk through the expectations process below. If the behavior is on the weightier side, then the boundaries and consequences need to be tough, and you need a therapist or pastor to walk you through what to do. However, if the behavior is on the lighter side, it is a matter of selfishness and immaturity. You need to still walk through the process below, but your intensity needs to be low. Why? Because you need to ask yourself, "What is the worst thing that happens if they don't clean off the counter after they make food? (Or leave their clothes on the floor, or doesn't tell you where they are going?)" The answer is NOT that it upsets you. What harm comes from it? The answer is either nothing or it is small, like you have to pick up their shirt. I am pointing this out to illustrate what I said above that it is not about the action itself; it is about what it *means* when they won't change. This is the core issue. If they won't change such a simple thing, what does that mean? They are immature, childish, selfish, etc., and that is truth.

Exposed

When your spouse/partner won't change, it drives you crazy and makes you angry, but why are you SO angry? What else does it mean to you? What emotional goal of yours is being blocked? Is it the emotional goal of being respected, desired, safe? We just stated that the actual consequences of their behaviors are minimal, so what's the big deal? You need to ask yourself what is being exposed in you. You need to dig and dig, don't stop, until you figure out why and what it is that is bothering you so much. The answer is going to be somewhere under the category of love. If they don't change, it must mean they don't love you, that they don't care about you, that you are not worth it, that you are not enough. Now, please listen carefully. All those things may be true and I am completely okay with concluding with those things because if they know they should change because their behavior is not RHWR and refuse to change (by their lack of change), then yes, they are being selfish and are showing you they don't care about you. However, what you need address is even though this is true, it may be pointing to an insecurity in you, or you take their lack of change personally, which means it is impacting your value and worth. Meaning, they are showing you that you are not important and worth it to them, but that doesn't mean that you are not important and not worth it. Does this make sense? The issue isn't that you aren't valuable and deserve to be loved, the issue is that you are that valuable and they are not treating you at the level of worth you deserve. If you struggle accepting this (be honest here, not defensive), you need to take time and read my first book but let me say that taking things personally impacts our value and worth. It is never a good idea to tie our value and worth to other people in our life. What does that mean? It means you *need* other people in your life to pursue you, validate you, do things for you. You need to solidify your identity, value, and worth enough to the point when you can say out of the confidence in your own heart that you don't *need* anyone to pursue you, validate you, or do things for you. You *want* them to, but you don't need them to. I can't emphasize how crucial it is for each of us to do this because the amount of emotional energy produced from these unfulfilled expectations becomes inflated, and we dump this emotional energy on our spouses, thus causing a lot of damage. We scream, "I need you to pick up after yourself or I won't feel loved by you, and I *need* to feel loved by you or I will be emotionally devasted and will wonder why I am not worth being loved!" Now we obviously don't say that verbally to our partner, but our unconscious selves are *screaming* that to our partner. After we go through the process of solidifying our identity, value, and worth, we can stay in the adult mode of the discussion (discussed next) and address the issue with our spouse at the right level of intensity. We would say, "I have asked you to change this behavior over and over, with no change on your part. When you don't change, you are absolutely communicating to me that I am not important to you, which hurts. However, this is not my issue, this is yours. Something is going on inside of you that you need to address, and until you do, you need to know that we are not okay, and our relationship is suffering because of it. Even though the issue is small, at this point, the real issue has been revealed: you are selfish. The things I keep asking you to change aren't the real issue; the issue is when you know you need to change and don't, it is because you are being selfish and immature. That is the issue we are dealing with here." Do you see the difference? Which one is more powerful? Which one has the greatest chance of producing change? If our intensity is way too high and we are causing damage, we need to walk into our negative emotions, figure out why, and deal with our insecurities and value and worth issues first. If not, the relationship will continue to dissolve and create trauma in both of you.

Now let's walk through the process of how to think through and address unfulfilled expectations. Again, all negative emotion is a result of unfulfilled expectations. Before we just sound off on our partners, we must do some internal work first. Here are the steps to walk yourself through:

Step 1: When you are angry or upset at what someone did/did not do, it is because of unfulfilled expectations. What happened that you did not expect to happen? What didn't happen that you expected to happen? What exactly were those expectations? Specify in your mind and then ask the person. "I expected or did not expect you to………..?"

Step 2: Ask yourself, "Were the expectations rational?" If they weren't, then the process ends because your partner didn't do anything wrong. If your expectations were rational, then go to step three.

Step 3: Did I clearly communicate my expectations to my partner? If not, then simply communicate your expectations. If you say, "They should have known," then be honest and ask if that is really RHWR to ensure you aren't just being critical. If the answer is "yes", then ask:

Step 4: Does my partner still agree? This may seem odd, but there are multiple times when a partner agrees to the expectations just to agree, but after thinking about it, they actually don't agree, but conveniently fail to communicate their change of heart with you. Simply ask, "Do you still agree with these expectations? If not, why?"

Step 5: Is there a RHWR reason why they didn't fulfill the agreed upon expectations? Believe it or not, there are times when legitimately "stuff happens" and your partner had every intention to fulfill them, but honestly couldn't. If nothing prohibited them fulfilling the expectations, then they should just use Instant Validation and own their mistake.

The main driving force behind this process is when the same expectation is unfulfilled over, and over, and over again. All the questions above have been answered in the affirmative except the last one where the partner has given every "the dog ate my homework" excuse in the book. They also commit the fundamental attribution error and point to their circumstances as the culprit behind the unfulfilled expectations.

Over time, intensity greatly increases because all the above happens, but the person continues not to fulfill the agreed-upon expectations. The person confronting feels like the other person is lying to them, ignoring them, not caring about what they think, etc. The person being confronted feels judged, parented, and defensive. When we continue to increase our intensity, our responses then start failing the RHWR test, and we start causing damage to the relationship. Our partner then shifts the topic of conversation from their continual failure to fulfill expectations to the topic of your emotional intensity. Using the non-RHWR pathway of intense communication very rarely achieves the goal, so we need to find a different path. If this is the case, then shift back to the adult role and ask, "What do we have to do different? What do you want me to do when this happens again? You equip me with the most effective response to you when you choose to break your promise again." Their suggestion needs to be RHWR, so make sure it is. We are tempted to go to the other extreme and just give up on the expectation, but that isn't healthy or right. You need to accept the fact that uncomfortable tension needs to be present until the partner fulfills the expectation. If there is a long-standing, consistent pattern of your partner not fulfilling agreed-upon expectations, you can say, "I hate this, but we are not okay. Our relationship is going to continue to suffer, and tension needs to continue to exist between us until you fulfill your promise. The issue isn't my intensity, the issue is you failing to keep your promise." Using the grace and truth principle, you can say, "I am not trying to judge, condemn, or parent you; I am trying to motivate you to change, hence the tension." If the unfulfilled expectation is more severe (like an addiction), such as the husband's continued use of pornography or the wife's ongoing abuse of alcohol, then the tension needs to turn into a formal separation of the relationship. It can start with the partner sleeping in a separate bedroom for one night, three nights, etc. or until there is an effort of "sobriety" from the behavior for a certain period. The length of time can start small, and you can add time every week or two until you determine the next phase to be that the partner needs to go and stay with a friend or family member after each failure, increasing the time of separation until eventually, it turns into full-time separation. This is a difficult process, and you should have already started counseling by this point. Work with your therapist and get wisdom on how to set tangible boundaries to increase the pain until the partner starts to feel that the pain of the consequences outweighs the emotional reward of the non-RHWR behaviors.

Stop and Schedule

Stop and Schedule should be used when either partner starts to realize that they are starting to get the point of no return, which means one or both are getting emotional enough where they won't be able self-regulate and are in danger of causing further damage to the relationship. This technique is the "fail safe" for either person to use to make sure they stop before they reach the point of no return. I have found that one partner practices "stopping" the argument, but when one spouse pulls away, states they need to think, or not talk about it anymore, the other spouse escalates because they feel like their partner is passive-aggressively saying, "Talk to the hand!" Normally, each relationship has a passive problem-solver (normally the introvert), and an active problem-solver (normally the extrovert) who wants to keep talking until the problem is solved. To achieve both goals, I have the couple use the **Stop and Schedule** technique. Technically, the partner who wants to stop the argument is doing a good thing, but he or she must satisfy the partner's goal with an exact time to revisit the topic. When either partner wants to stop the argument, then they *must schedule a specific time to come back and solve the problem.* The time can either be in 15 minutes, a half-hour, two hours, etc. Or it can be a different day/time, such as tomorrow at 7:00 p.m. or Sunday at 3:00. When you do this, both can achieve their goals. ***When you do come back together, then use either Couple's/Empathy Dialogue or the RHWR problem-solving technique described below to ensure that you don't escalate again!***

Richer Communication

Being a Safe Sounding Board
A classic mistake of a husband is to try and fix his wife's problems when she is venting. The wife is experiencing the conversation as the *Her Needs* pathway of Intimate Conversation to accomplish

the emotional goal of security. Because many husbands see all negative emotions problems to be solved, and from their philosophy of *happy wife, happy life*, they try and fix their wife's problem, not realizing her goal is connection, not getting a solution to her problems. However, there are times when the husband wants to vent as well and is not looking for advice but just wants to vent. The following techniques I give to executives I coach to help them be great listeners with their followers. The first technique is the common skill of paraphrasing, or empathy. *Restate, using synonyms, what you heard your spouse say they are feeling, and repeat the facts to their story. Restate not only the explicit message (actual words spoken), but also the implicit message (not actually spoken, but definitely a factor impacting the story). Use the format, "You're (emotions), because of (facts, details, story)."* For example, *"You're frustrated because your mom never seems to compliment you or validate you, but only correct you."* Chances are, we've all heard of this technique, but almost all of us are very poor at using it! This technique would be good for every single person on Earth to master and use frequently in conversation.

The second technique to master is to *replace giving advice with asking questions*. Think of questions in the categories of past, present, future. You can ask questions about the past, such as the chronology of events that led up to the current situation. On the present, you can ask questions about what your partner is currently feeling and all the implications of the situation. The most important is asking questions about the future. This is where you turn your advice into questions. Instead of saying, "You need to email them and tell them that they need to . . .!" Instead of this forceful, non-empathic approach, turn it into a question. Ask, "What do you think is best? Are you going to email them to lay out the issue clearly or do you think it's better to meet face-to-face?" Whether it be your husband or wife, or frankly, anyone else, paraphrase what the person is saying and ask questions instead of giving advice!

Couple's (or Empathy) Dialogue
This technique is a much more thorough version of the paraphrasing technique above. Whenever a couple needs to discuss a topic that is sensitive, emotional, or easily gets escalated, I suggest using this technique. Per usual, use the exact name of the skill to achieve pattern interruption. This process is going to seem very foreign and mechanical, but that is the point; it is to force the couple from going about their normal patterns. Additionally, the goal of this technique is *not* to problem-solve, it is to *feel heard* by one another. I have a couple of techniques below to help with problem-solving, but I also tell couples that most of them are smart enough to simply solve a non-emotional problem. The goal is for each person to feel heard and to keep the conversation from shooting off into other tangential topics. Picture this technique like a funnel. You both start at the top, feeling far apart on the issue, and as you use this technique, you will move to the bottom of the funnel and have this feeling of "okay, now what?" That feeling comes from the fact that you understand one another now, so you can start problem-solving. Here are the steps:

- To start, person 1 gets three to five sentences to open the discussion. Anyone can start. You only get three to five sentences because your partner will have to paraphrase what you said. When you only have three-to-five sentences, you are much more selective in your word choice. The other thing I find is you have a hard time knowing where to begin. This is because you have probably had this conversation several times before. Just pick the sentences and begin, the conversation will get rolling, I promise you!

- Person 2 paraphrases what their partner said, using synonyms (not parroting their exact words) by starting with, "So what you are saying is….." ***The most important piece of this technique is after paraphrasing, they MUST end with "Am I getting it?"*** This is where the technique rises or falls. ***It is illegal (you will be arrested) for you to come back with your opinion until you get a "yes" from your partner on the question, "Am I getting it?"***
- You want the person to say, "Yes, absolutely." If they pause, you got part of it, but not all of it. They will clarify again, and then person 2 will have to restate again. Person 2 will have to continue to restate until person 1 says "Yes."
- Person 2 then gets three to five sentences to say whatever they want in response to what person 1 said. The same guidelines above apply.
- The process goes back and forth until both feel heard to the point that there is a feeling of "Okay, now what?" Once you get there, then you can do simple problem-solving. It looks like this:

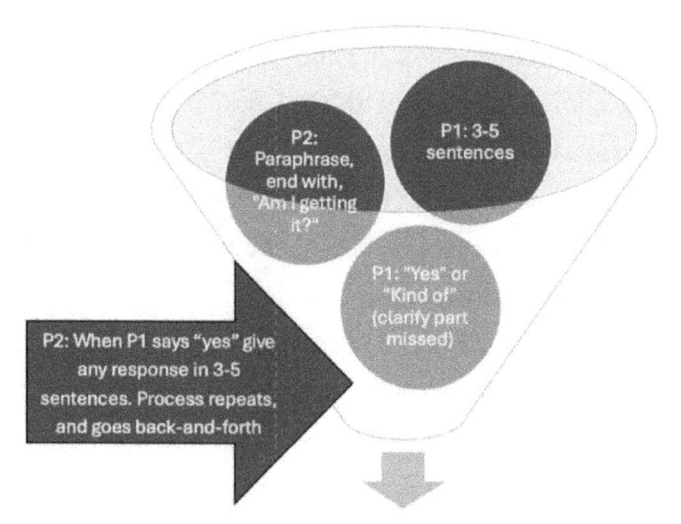

Both feel heard, then use problem-solving skills. What's the solution?

Problem-Solving Skills

Moving Forward

This technique flows from the problem above when couples try and prove the past with he said/she said, he did/she did, as well as the whole debate over how the other person came across. When a couple starts getting sucked down the drain of those fruitless conversations, I interrupt them and say, "Just say, 'Moving forward, let's agree to do this differently . . .'" It may seem simple, but if I had a dollar for every time a couple needed that one shift to be able to stop their arguing, I'd be a rich man!

Multiple Goals, Multiple Paths – Using RHWR in problem-solving

Whenever there is a disagreement between two people on a certain topic, such as how much to spend on Christmas presents, they try and win the argument and use whatever evidence or points they can to prove their partner is in the wrong. After the argument, I have them take a break and ask themselves out of everything they said, what is the main point to their argument? Then, I ask them to pull out the main point from their spouse's argument. Instead of burning a lot of emotional energy on where their partner is wrong, how their partner is immature, where their character is flawed, and their evil motives, they need to discipline themselves and ask, "What is my main point? Is my main point RHWR? What is their main point? Is their main point RHWR?" 99% of the time, the actual main points will pass the RHWR test. Using the budget for Christmas as an example, one spouse wants to achieve the emotional goal of making it the best Christmas ever while the other spouse wants to stay within the budget. Is there a way to accomplish both goals?

Once they pull out the main points, they will then begin to realize that they made several tangential, non-RHWR statements *that orbited around their main points*. When they come back together, they need to validate and clarify each other's main points and then "own" the facts by stating what statements they made to one another that were not RHWR. Once they do that, then they can go to the third step and problem-solve by coming up with the most RHWR solution to each other's main points.

As soon as a disagreement appears, immediately know that each person has a main point, or you can even turn that main point into goals. Often, when we make a point, we will say, "I'm fine with that as long as . . ." and what immediately follows is the partner's main point or main goal. Whenever there is a disagreement, you know there is more than one goal we need to achieve. For example, a common (silly) argument spouses have is when they are trying to decide where they should go out to eat. What are the emotional goals? To feel full and to have a pleasurable experience as the food passes over our palette, accompanied by someone we love.

When arguing about the relatives coming over, one spouse will say, "I am fine with them coming over, as long as I don't have to hear about how we aren't doing a good job as parents!" The original idea could've been not having them over, but that obviously wouldn't work! So, there are two goals: 1. Have an ongoing relationship with the relatives, and 2. Agree on how to set appropriate boundaries or have an effective response when they criticize your parenting. When it comes to our relatives, here are two techniques I give to help with those wonderful relatives!

Two Techniques to Reclaim the Power

The "Have Faith" Technique

Do you have anyone in your life that drives you crazy, that is to say, someone who is always making comments and arguing with you. I want you to have faith, and I'm not just talking about faith in God. How many times have you began a sentence in your mind with, "I can't believe they . . ."? How many times have you began a sentence that way when you think about them? Well, start believing; have faith. The fact that you are still shocked they say what they say or do what they do is kind of more of your issue, not theirs, right? The technique starts with changing the time direction of your emotional energy. Instead of processing what they *did*, think ahead and predict what they are going to do or say. If you have a spouse or sibling who shares your grief, team up with them and make dollar bets with one another. Think ahead to the next interaction you will have with that person and start brainstorming what you think they will say or do if any given topic comes up. If the topic of your children comes up, what will they say? You will say, "I think they will say . . ." and your spouse/sibling will say, "No, I think they will say . . .". Well, bet on it. When the time comes and that person puts their lack of emotional intelligence on full display, what do you think your auto-response will be at that moment? First, before you even complete your statement or response, you will have gleeful anticipation, excited to see who's right. When the person acts their usual way, you will either say, "Yes! I was right!" or "Shoot! I thought I had that one!" That person will be confused and all you have to say is, "Sorry, inside joke!" Prepare by considering what the most RHWR response would be if they respond with option A and the most RHWR response if they respond with option B. Be careful not to strategize on what the greatest "burn" comeback would be, although tempting, but the most effective, RHWR response.

    Our goal here is not to win an insult contest but respond in the most effective way, the most emotionally intelligent way, and the most RHWR way. Think back to Chapter One and achieve the two goals of grace and truth. Make sure your response is like a grace-truth-grace response. You can say something like, "I understand your frustration, but the truth is . . . but I can see your point too." Think about the difference in the emotional experience before and after using this technique. You have completely taken the power that person had over you to trigger you emotionally, and now are completely equipped to minimize the person's impact on you. Whatever those people have said, it was probably exposing some insecurity in you, whether what they said contained some element of truth or contained no truth. Either way, it drove you crazy, right? Why? You don't have any control over them; you only have control over your intrapersonal and interpersonal responses.

As an example, I often work with couples who have an aging parent who makes a lot of critical comments every time they are with them. This happens a lot during the holidays and is frankly the reason why the holidays can be so stressful! The comments can come in various forms, and seemingly come out of the blue, and the feeling is that the comments are completely unnecessary. Sometimes the comment is a true statement about what you did, such as "Well, she didn't try very hard in high school" or "I always told him he needed to find a career that made more money". Both statements are factually true and pass the RHWR test. So why does it trigger us so bad? The principles in the chapter on insecurity apply here, but they may not because you have no problem "owning" the truth of those statements. What creates the emotion and why if feels like your parent is "pushing your buttons" is the *meaning and motive behind the statements*. Why do these people make these statements? Whenever we explain it by saying, "she is just trying to . . ." we are trying to assess the meaning and motive behind the comments. Honestly, the specific motive is irrelevant, but no matter what, one of the emotional goals of the person, especially if it's a parent, is to highlight their strengths as a parent, or to have the feeling of being an effective parent (by continuing to try and parent). Remind yourself over and over that any critique done in a non-RHWR way is all about the person trying to achieve their own emotional goal, and ultimately is not about you. Use this technique to remove all power from the environment (the one critiquing), because the principles in the chapter on insecurity apply here. We can truly get to the point where we have NO insecurities. The other type of comments come in the form of generalizations, such as, "you need to be more organized," or "your children need more love from you," or "if you put in more effort, things would go your way". These generalizations can easily set us off only way to prove it true is to give several examples, but then everyone gets lost in arguing over the details of the examples. It is impossible to prove generalizations wrong ... impossible, because most generalizations are a mixture of truth and untruths. With generalizations, I have learned to either just say, "That's true" or if I want to have fun with it, I use the following technique.

Embrace the "Digs"
What do you do when people make comments that are simply a one-liner insult or "dig"? I have had people in my life who did this. I remember going absolutely insane each time they would throw that grenade in my direction. Using the "exposed" principle, I kept asking myself what was being exposed in me and would hold myself accountable and say to myself, "Greg, the fact that you get so upset when they do that is not their issue, it's yours. Why are

you giving them so much power over you?" When people use these one-liners against us, it is so easy to start attacking their character and motives. Many of those judgments may have some merit, but is attacking them in our minds the most RHWR path to achieve the emotional goal of confidence and security? Of course not, but that is such a common path we use, with very little fruit at the end. The most effective technique I created was to respond to their digs by embracing and even exaggerating them. I didn't even bother trying to differentiate with them whether what they said was true or not true, I simply would agree. For example, if someone said to me when I was in ministry, "Well, a more seasoned pastor wouldn't do that" I would simply say, "Oh my goodness, you are right. I have some serious immaturity issues! I'm surprised the Board of Elders haven't called me in to address it with me!" When you agree with it and even extrapolate, they are left speechless because you have completely sucked all the negative energy and power out of the comment. After, they don't have any more emotional fuel to keep it going. When I began practicing that technique, the results were amazing. It made the situation lighter, and many times, we both laughed. Try it! Now, if what they said had merit, I would absolutely walk away owning it and trying to work on it. If it wasn't true, then it ended right there. I simply quit walking down the pathway of defending myself, trying to convince someone else to think differently of me. However, it always depends on the person. Sometimes, I would respond with this technique and if their comment was out of character for them, I would follow up and ask them if there was something we needed to talk about. I used the Proactive Teachability technique to remove their defensive mechanisms because maybe they were seeing something I don't. This technique is more effective for those people who have an addiction to just lobbing grenades of criticism with no real desire to problem-solve or make the relationship stronger. Just like in the technique above, the emotional goal of the person throwing these grenades of insults is to feel more confident, significant, etc., so changing them or having them stop launching the grenades is simply an unachievable goal and I quit trying to achieve it. Insecurity is at the bottom level of my emotional management system. Our insecurities are always present and may be exposed at any minute.

CHAPTER 7:

SCHEDULING THE MINIMUM

His left hand is under my head, and his right hand embraces me.

– Song of Songs 2:6

The second phase of counseling is *scheduling the minimum*, and I explained the underlying rationale and philosophy in chapter five. Now, I want to give you the five components of scheduling the minimum and how to apply each one. I love bragging to couples that I have given this system to hundreds and hundreds of couples over the years, and after explaining it, I ask, "If you did these five things regularly, would you have enough time together, and would your relationship be healthy and thrive?" Every couple I have worked with has emphatically said, "Yes!" Well, maybe the wife has been more enthusiastic than the man, which is not a "diss" to the wife, as if she is more needy. She is more enthusiastic because she finally has a quantifiable process to which the husband agrees, so she doesn't have to continue to plead with him anymore. I also point out to the husband that having this "checklist" also allows him the peace of mind that he'll be meeting his wife's needs in that area. It's freeing for both the husband and wife. Like communication skills, I ask the couple to commit to practicing this system because, as I stated earlier, negative emotions come from unfulfilled expectations. If this system is practiced, then many of the arguments we have as couples quit occurring. This system ensures that one another's expectations are specific, discussed, agreed upon, and hopefully fulfilled. Being in sync like this gives much needed emotional relief from the constant bickering, therefore, generating the beautiful feeling of teamwork and partnership. It clears the emotional obstacles that were in the way of us pursuing each other, boosting momentum for the couple to continue up the number line. The same concept can be used with respect to quality time with our children. I will go deeper into some parenting techniques later, but the key principle with scheduling the minimum with our children is intentionality. As parents, it is easy to get complacent because our relationships are filled with wonderful memories from birth through preschool. As many of us know, everything changes "overnight" when our children go through puberty. Suddenly, we go from being their heroes to being the nerdy kid they want to bully. If your children are still in middle school, then start implementing this principle now. When it comes to being intentional, throw you and your children into the future and ask, "What do I want to be able to say about our parenting when our children are gone? What do I want my children to say about our parenting? I want them to say we were intentional and strategic as parents, so what would that look like?" A little forewarning: what you want your children to say about your parenting and what they will actually say will be completely different. What we would consider as defining moments in their childhood, they don't even remember, and what we don't even remember sticks with them forever. In their 20s, they seem to tease us, and it feels like the only thing they remember is how rough they had it. I have told my children, "Man, I didn't realize how crappy of a dad I was!" They are just teasing, but it is surprising what they remember and what impacted them the most. Don't worry, and just wait. When they have children, we will start to become the wise sage who sits on top of the mountain!

To achieve the goals of intentionality and scheduling the minimum, consider the goal you want to achieve. Think about it, what do parents lament about with their children? That they don't open up enough and we don't know what is *really* going on with our kids. I have heard some parents brag that they know their kids inside and out, only to find out later how little they knew! Remember, every relationship is about safety and pursuit. We want our children to feel completely safe with us to be able to open up about what is going on with their lives, and we want our children to say they feel pursued by us. Please greatly lower your expectations during the teenage years about your children returning the favor and give up on trying to *feel* pursued by your teen. It's okay, and that is my point: the need for intentionality. In middle school, schedule a time with each child, let's say every other week, when both of you will go into your child's bedroom, close the door, and just talk about what is going on in each of your lives (model transparency and openness to them, some kids don't know how to do it). I advise going into their bedroom because that is their safe zone (as opposed to your bedroom or another room in the house), and *your presence in their room helps them remember that their room is on loan from you; it's your house. Further, it helps them remember your presence when they are tempted to do things they shouldn't do. There is something powerful about them experiencing your relational presence in their room. Trust me, your aura is left behind after these meetings, and that is a good thing.*

When it comes to pursuit, schedule a dad/daughter, dad/son, mom/daughter, mom/son date once every month or so (depending on how many kids, schedules, etc.). The minimum is not a law, it's a principle. What would be the minimum? I encourage individual dates because 1) we need individual time with each of them, 2) they need individual time with each of us, 3) we act differently when we are with our spouse, so going on individual dates frees us more (it's okay, it's a good thing), and 4) our children act and engage differently with each parent and has a different chemistry with each parent. I hope you are nodding your head right now, but you are also probably a little overwhelmed by the number of events and time involved. That is why the intentionality is so important!

Please listen to me right now.

You know the impact of doing this with each child, but you are all so busy. Listen, each family must take a serious look at their schedules. We all have a certain number of slices in our life pies, and each slice **must** be allotted the minimum amount of time to achieve our macro-emotional goal of the highest quality of life. Our highest quality of life is divided into the standard of living (working hard to earn enough money for our needs and to enjoy life), living our values (proof of what we truly value is our schedules and bank accounts, own it), and our destiny (calling, purpose, vision, and legacy). Scheduling the minimum is NOT just about time management, although it is a powerful technique if we use it. This is about getting out of the weeds of micro-emotional goals, which are led by our passivity and impulsive decision-making, being ruled by the whirlwind of our culture. Many of us have values that we to live but they are not already ingrained in our mental models, so we need a way to create formulas in our mental models that have these values incorporated into the formula. It's simple training via repetition, and that repetition happens when we regularly practice it and the way we regularly practice it is to be constantly reminded of it and the way we are constantly reminded of it is by having it as a recurring event in our calendars. We need to get to a 30,000-foot view of our lives and do some serious evaluation of how well we are achieving our macro-emotional goals (values, beliefs, philosophy of life). However, give you and your spouse grace because I have found that it takes weeks and sometimes months to implement this process. Not only that, we need to adjust and re-evaluate every season, because each season has its own unique opportunities and challenges. It's a process but be relentless about implementing it.

The Five Areas of Scheduling the Minimum in Our Marriage

Daily Connect
Because life is so busy, take time once a day during the week to just sit down together and ask, "How was your day?" Normally, it would happen after work, before dinner. Just stop, sit on the couch, and connect. Remember goal vs. path. The goal is to connect daily and touch base on what is going on, what each person needs to

know, and walk through one another's life experiences over the last 24 hours. The path needs to match your schedules. The ideal time is after work before dinner, but if the goal is to connect daily (and ensure you don't become the proverbial two ships passing in the night) then practice this whenever it works for the two of you.

Daily Deeper Connect

I have found couples, among all the other "couple" things, want to grow together. When you first met, you were attracted to each other, so you started dating. When you were dating, you discussed everything under the sun and found that you had a lot of common interests. These interests weren't just recreational in nature; they were deeper and in line with the macro-emotional goals. You discussed your jobs, desired standard of living, life values in all areas, your philosophy of life, why you are here, which is all about your destiny, calling, purpose, and legacy. Once you discovered you were aligned enough there, you really started to entertain the idea that you had found our person, and now you *really* couldn't wait until the wedding night to get this party started. Once you begin your lives together, you need to be intentional about continuing to grow together. Growing together can take shape in many forms: reading books together, discussing how to achieve our macro-emotional goals, setting personal development goals.

For Christian couples, I immediately start asking about their plan for leading the family physically. Are you reading the Bible and praying together? Here is where I speak directly to husbands. Any husband who has been a Christian long enough will hear that we need to lead our family spiritually. This is an area of incredible weakness in our Christian homes. Don't worry! No guilt trip! I desperately want to encourage and equip husbands to be successful in this area. The main obstacle I find in men has to do with their main emotional goal of significance. Men are always pursuing ways to feel successful and significant, which is great. However, if we are honest guys, we also avoid topics that make us feel insignificant. Many men don't feel they are godly enough, know the Bible enough, or don't have the entire Bible memorized in the original languages of Hebrew, Aramaic, and Greek, consequently they don't feel equipped to lead their families spiritually. However, guys, you *know* that leading your families spiritually is not contingent upon you feeling competent to lead.

The Theology of Spiritual Leadership

When you think back to the fall of man in Genesis 3, who disobeyed God first, Adam or Eve? Eve did. So why does Romans 5:12 blame Adam for thrusting humanity into sin? It states, "Therefore, just as sin entered the world through one man, and death through sin, and in this way death came to all people, because all sinned."[7] The reason why is found in 2 Timothy 2 when the Apostle Paul is explaining that men should be the spiritual leaders in the church, and the reasons he states are 1) the fact that Adam was formed first, then Eve (v. 13). Here, he uses a universal (not cultural or situational) reason for men to be spiritual leaders, 2) he states that Adam wasn't the one deceived, but Eve was deceived and fell into

---

[7] Holy Bible, New International Version®, NIV® Copyright © 1973, 1978, 1984, 2011 by Biblica, Inc

disobeying. But wait! That declaration is not a criticism of Eve but of Adam. If you go back and read the account of the garden, you will see that Satan had to talk Eve into disobeying, which he did by telling her a number of lies. She did not get the command not to eat the forbidden fruit directly from God but heard it from Adam. So, when Satan lied to her, she believed the lies and ate the fruit. Adam was right there, was passive in his leadership, and she gave him the fruit too, and he ate it.

In the Old Testament, there are descriptions of *intentional* sins and *unintentional* sins. We can commit unintentional sins by being deceived or ignorant of a rule, but intentional sins are when we know it's wrong and do it anyway. It's rebellion. Eve's sin was unintentional, while Adam's sin was intentional. Adam was created first and was meant to lead. God directly told him the command, and Adam flat out disobeyed after being told to lead the family back to God. In Ephesians 5, the Apostle Paul told husbands that they are to bathe their marriage in the word of God, and later in Ephesians 6, he told fathers to bring their children up in the training and admonition of the Lord. Biblically, we know men must lead spiritually in the church and the family.

A man's need to feel significant and his duty to lead the family spiritually is often hindered because many men don't feel like they know the Bible well enough to lead and teach the family. However, husbands and fathers, what is the goal here? The goal is to *lead* (influence) the family spiritually. I tell husbands and fathers there are two ways for them to do this: 1) Influence via example, 2) leadership via initiation. Men lead their families via influence whenever his wife and children can say it's obvious that he loves the Lord. Guys, what would you have to do in order for your family to say it's obvious you love the Lord? Then do that. Second, leadership is about taking the lead and initiating the things that should be done as believers. Initiate and make sure you are reading the Bible with your wife and children. When you have dinner together, just read one chapter while the family is eating. Initiate a process for your children to have their own personal time with the Lord. Initiate and make sure your family goes to church, is involved in ministry, and is part of a small group within the church.

After having this conversation with countless families, I am confident some of you may be thinking of all the obstacles in your way. If you literally can't do any of the above, then your family has major priority issues. Own it. Additionally, don't fall into an "all or nothing" mindset. Maybe some days you fall off track and don't make time for spirituality. Aim for four out of seven days a week of reading the Bible so you can say that most days, you open up the Word with your family. Finally, I like asking individuals a few questions. Is it obvious to you and others that Jesus is your First Love (Revelation 2:4)? You know that answer and what to do if the answer is no. When it comes to devotion and commitment to the Lord, would the Lord describe you as hot, cold or lukewarm (Revelation 3:16)? You know that answer and what to do if the answer is no. Have you left all to follow Him (Luke 14:26)? You know that answer and what to do if the answer is no. I believe there are two decisions we must make in our response to Jesus. To believe in what He did on the cross to pay for our sins (salvation), and the very separate decision where we first must sit down and count the cost to truly be His disciple (Luke 14). Men and women, the choice is yours. (what about mentioning here about the impact it has on the kids?)

Date Night Once per Week
Every couple knows this should be non-negotiable. When it comes to date night, there have been some common patterns I have seen across marriages throughout the years. The first pattern is the shift from romance, infatuation, fun, and lightheartedness during the dating and engagement periods to the "mode" of being roommates and business partners after the honeymoon, as the couple is trying to achieve the tangible components of our highest quality of life (our standard of living, for example). All couples need to be reminded that their highest quality of life must also include the intangible aspects (values, beliefs, philosophy). When we stop for a minute, we know in our hearts that at the end of our lives, the only thing we will care about and reflect on are our relationships and our legacy of living our true values. The relationship and romance of a young couple culminates at the altar and then once they get back from the honeymoon, the reality of real life makes them pour most of their emotional energy into being roommates and business partners. Almost every couple believes in having regular date nights, but they forget to get out of roommate and business partner mode for the date! When they sit down for dinner, they impulsively think of topics of discussion, start talking about calendar stuff, finances, parenting, etc., and then get into an argument, killing the vibe of a date night. How many of you have experienced this?

To ensure date nights are what they are supposed to be, I suggest the couple schedule a business time once per week as well, which

I will discuss next. If any problem comes up during date night, either partner can set a boundary and remind their partner they can discuss it during business time. There are three goals of date night: have fun, flirt, and show affection. As a matter of fact, the success of the date should be measured by how well you achieved these three goals. These were the three things we absolutely mastered when we won our spouse to the alter in the first place. When you hear that marriage is hard work, I don't believe it has to do with arguing; it is about working hard to keep the relationship fresh and fun. If you noticed, I did not say that the success of a date is measured by where you went out to eat. As I stated earlier, ridiculous arguments can start when discussing where to eat. For dates, I believe that there should be mutual pursuit. I have couples taking turns planning the dates. One week it's the husband's duty, the next week it is the wife's duty. They take turns planning where they are going to eat and the activity they are going to do, you don't ask if it's okay, you just do it. There are a million ideas on both, so just put some thought into it and plan it. You can make what you do on the dates centered around those things and throw axes, do a painting activity, or simply have a picnic. When each of you take turns, it is mutual pursuit, more thought is put into it, making it more creative, and it keeps the relationship fresh.

Weekly Business Time

The success of scheduling the minimum rises and falls on being consistent in weekly business times. There are four roles couples fulfill with one another: roommates, business partners, friends, and lovers. I strongly advise couples not to drag the first two into the feelings associated with the second two. If your husband still isn't good at cleaning off the counter after they make themselves some food and hasn't after countless times of asking does not mean they don't love you, they are just a pig. It's a roommate issue. Additionally, we must realize that we are also business partners. When you married, you didn't just become a couple, you started a process that will potentially last over 50 years. You began the process of building our estates. Your children, their education, your grandchildren, their marriages, your financial portfolio, your retirement, and on and on it goes. You need to have weekly staff meetings to plan, strategize, discuss how to be the most successful in your "careers" of your family.

Once a week, schedule one hour to go over calendars, finances, parenting, and discussion topics you need to discuss. Use a shared calendar, create a recurring appointment, and in the notes section of that appointment, put the agenda I just gave. During the week, either spouse can open up the upcoming business time and add items to the agenda. Under the calendar, have the first two items be date night and business time. Many couples are unable to meet at the same day and time, so schedule the next four weeks ahead of time for date and business times. Next, add other items that need to get scheduled, like the next visit to grandma's, you can also discuss details, logistics, and expectations for upcoming events. Who will drop off and pick up little Billy? With events, agree ahead of time that when you go over to the Stewart's Friday night for dinner, you will leave by 11:00 p.m. because "you know how Greg gets!" When you get detailed and specific, it saves you from a lot of arguments, just with calendar items. Further, you add specific upcoming topics to discuss under finances, parenting, and current relational topics in the marriage. If a topic is sensitive or heavy, use the communication techniques of couple's dialogue or the RHWR problem-solving process, where you clearly define one another's main points.

There's one major point I need to make about budgets. Couple's consistently only focus on the monthly budget, income, and expenses. If the income is greater than expenses and you have $500 left over at the end of the month, you need to put that towards the second budget that no one seems to consider: the annual budget. The annual budget are the items of emergency funds, Christmas, new clothes, birthdays, car maintenance, health care costs, quarterly getaways (discussed next), and vacations. If you have roughly $500 left over at the end of each month, then that means you have an annual budget of $6,000 to use on all the items I just listed. How much money will you spend on Christmas this year? Vacation? What about birthdays? Once you buy your mom a present and take her out to dinner, you just spent $150. How many of those do you have per year? Finances are obviously a well-known point of contention for couples. I remind couples that numbers are black-and-white, they are unemotional, and they don't budge. Whatever your desired quality of life, it is absolutely limited by these numbers. With the monthly budget, the discussion is either how to increase income or decrease expenses. The discussion for the annual budget is what to earmark the discretionary income for when you transfer it over to the savings account. Once the monthly and annual budget is set up, it doesn't take much time to go over it each week, but this system saves a lot of arguments.

Quarterly Getaways

The fifth component of scheduling the minimum is quarterly getaways. I advise the couple to schedule a weekend getaway once per quarter. Get out of town, get a hotel or VRBO, make reservations for a great dinner Friday night and Saturday night, sleep in on Saturday, go shopping or do an activity on Saturday, take a nap, and take your passion to the next level. While I encourage the couple to take turns planning date nights, one spouse is normally better at planning quarterly getaways, so it's okay if one partner assumes management over this. However, if one of the getaways is around that partner's birthday, then the other partner needs to step up and plan it. I am better at planning these weekends and love doing it. My wife and I have been very consistent at quarterly getaways and have absolutely loved them. It is so much fun and relaxing and allows us a beautiful time to empty our stress out and reconnect.

Question: if you did these five things as a couple, would you have enough time together and would your relationship be healthy and thrive? I thought so.

CHAPTER 8:

I HAVE NEVER BEEN LOVED LIKE THIS BEFORE

Your lips are like a strand of scarlet, and your mouth is lovely.

– Song of Songs 4:3

The final phase of marriage counseling is to equip the couple to truly experience the type of love relationship that God intended when he created marriage, which is exemplified in the book of the Bible, Song of Songs. This book is an absolute love romance between King Solomon and his wife. It is also a reflection of the type of love relationship between Christ and His church. God calls Himself the bridegroom and His church is the bride. He loves us more than we could ever imagine. Every romantic movie you have watched, any story that made your throat swell and eyes flood with the power of love, originated in the heart of God. There was a documentary recently created about near-death experiences, called *After Death*. I cannot overemphasize your need to watch this film. The one life-changing takeaway I had from the film was the account every person recounted when they stood before Christ and God. The light and love that flowed from their presence melted those who stood exposed to it. They all made this one startling statement in describing that moment, "I felt as if I was the only person in the universe God loved."

My dear, dear friend, when God created marriage, his intent was we would say that very thing about both our Creator and our spouse. As I stated, we are to maximize our safety to emulate the type of emotional and relational safety the Trinity experiences. With pursuit, we are to maximize that pursuit with our spouse to the point where we say that we feel that we have never been loved like this before. There are only two of us on Earth in marriage, and the third member of our Trinity is to be the Lord God himself. You may have heard this "trinity" to be likened to a triangle, with God at the top and each partner at the other two points on the bottom. As we grow closer to God, we grow closer to each other.

In my first book, I talk about my personal journey of creating intimacy with the Lord. Out of my own insecurities that culminated in an emotional affair, I began the journey of going both inward and upward. I had to face my deepest emotions inwardly, facing them and walking right into them. Simultaneously, I pushed upward into my relationship with the Lord. I stepped back and observed all of humanity's struggle to find peace with their God. In Christianity, I saw the same thing; there were those who "got it" and they possessed the most tender, peaceful, love relationship with their Savior. I wanted that. In order to accomplish this, I began envisioning Jesus every time I prayed and would engage Him as my first love and fiancé. Instead of the common fears and awkwardness I felt when I began to pray, feeling sinful and dirty, I would picture walking into His presence and Him greeting me like my perfect fiancé would. His face would brighten with a smile, excited to see me and spend time with me. I did not forego my need for confession because it was His absolute love that reminded me how beautiful and perfect He was and how I did not honor that in so many ways throughout my day. I would confess, not out of an expression of being stained, but out of an expression of hurt because I wounded my fiancé's heart. He loves me and every time I sinned, I hurt his heart. I don't want to do that. I never want to sin again, but I do, and each time I walk into His presence I'm reminded that He is my first love and my fiancé and when I am in His presence, I feel like I am the only person in the universe He loves. His love compels me (2 Corinthians 5:14) to be holy, and to love, just like He loves me.

For our marriages, that kind of love is what each of us desire, not only to receive but to give. I could write volumes on the need for each of us to find peace with God. We will never be able to love our spouse until we have the same love and acceptance towards ourselves that God has towards us. I feel compelled to remind us that Jesus came full of grace and truth (John 1:14) and the same principle applies here that grace and empathy, without truth and boundaries, is enablement. Truth and boundaries without grace and empathy are toxic. It is the combination of both grace and truth that become our guiding ropes with which we grasp where the weaknesses of enablement and toxicity cannot take hold. We need to walk into the truth of our negative emotions and what they are exposing in us in order to face the things we need to face hiding in the basement of our hearts. We do this with the love, compassion, empathy, and grace given to us by our Savior. Only then can we grow, heal, rest, and find peace. There is a direct correlation, I have found, between our ability to do this and our ability to love our spouse's the way God intended.

The +6 to +10 zone is the fulfillment of Mark 10:45, "For the Son of Man did not come to be served, but to serve, and give his life as a ransom for many."[8] In this zone, I do everything I can to have the same mindset, that is why I said earlier it is a mindset of "I have no rights" and "Whatever my wife wants, she gets." We both try to out-serve one another. We look for ways to encourage one another, to serve one another, care for one another, and make each other's world better. Remember, pursuit is when we do a specific romantic action that creates a positive emotional experience in our partner. Search the internet for 101 ways to show my husband/wife I love them. Create a list of 15-20 ideas you can do to fulfill each of their love languages. It's not hard, people. The goal is consistency. What makes us love these things so much when our partner does them for us? It is because we don't expect it, because the texts, the statements, the notes, the gifts, and/or the pre-planned events come out of the blue. We love this because we realize that our spouse is thinking about us and how to express their love for us when we don't expect it. That's love. That's pursuit.

Thumper Ideas

In addition to the above, I have had couples think of things that are unique and specific to them and if your spouse initiated these things, you would transform into Thumper (from the movie

---

[8] Holy Bible, New International Version®, NIV® Copyright © 1973, 1978, 1984, 2011 by Biblica, Inc

Bambi). If your spouse did that for you, your leg would begin thumping uncontrollably out of absolute giddiness and ecstasy. These are the items that would fall under either *His Needs/Her Needs* or *The Five Love Languages*. Each of us can agree these lists capture how we'd love to be shown love by our spouse, but we each have specific actions under these items that would make us especially happy. Women love affection, honesty/openness, conversation, quality time, etc. but ladies, what *specifically* would you like your husbands to do within these categories? Husbands love their spouse to be attractive, physical touch, verbal affirmation, and admiration, but guys, what *specifically* would *you* absolutely love your wife to do under those catagories? I ask each spouse to email or text their spouse two or three of these Thumper ideas.

Do not tell them verbally. Why? Because some of the ideas are quirky or have a "fetish" component to them, and we could feel very embarrassed and exposed if we shared them. Worse than that, if we verbally share with our spouse these things to their face, their facial expression could trigger a judged emotion and could potentially make us absolutely shut down and "retreat back inside." We need to practice and maximize safety with one another. Some of you are very tender and apprehensive to open up with one another, so texting or emailing these ideas first and then discussing them later (ensuring we tell our spouses they are safe) would protect that transparency.

Now, I am sure every one of you noticed that I did not list sex as one of the men's topics. I have found that when I either discuss the idea of Thumper ideas or the concept of "Whatever my spouse wants, they get," women have recoiled at the idea, and they immediately must start throwing up iron border walls and begin shouting disclaimers and exceptions to the rules. Allow me to go a bit deeper here, because in the +6 to +10 zone, this isn't an issue of fear, but excitement. You won't see these fears and boundaries expressed in the Song of Songs! Here are some general points that guide this ever-sensitive topic:

1. Ladies don't assume that if you said to your husband, "Whatever you want, you get," he is immediately going to ask you to reenact *50 Shades of Grey*. Yes, there are some guys, *and* women, who do enjoy those things, but chances are your husband doesn't. Please don't believe the lie in your mind and use it as an excuse to withhold sexual expression. HOWEVER (sheez, I feel like I had to capitalize that because I just triggered half of you),
2. When it comes to sexual "expression," whatever is permissible for both is permissible, but if it's not permissible to one, it's not permissible to either. You both need to practice safety and discuss what is acceptable with both of you.
3. This is what I know to be true: many guys need to be more content in the degree of sexual expression by their wives, and many wives need to stretch themselves in their degree of sexual expression and not frame the entire topic as a threat to their emotional safety.

Guys, I believe the *only* way for our wives to be open to expressing themselves more is for them to experience the *brag about* status for an extended period of time. Maximization of safety is the pre-requisite before the maximization of pursuit. Ladies, if you can say of your husband, "I have never been loved like this before," then you need to do some inner work and figure out what is being exposed in you that is preventing you from the level of expression of Solomon's wife in the Song of Songs. For you, maximization of pursuit is a pre-requisite before the maximization of safety. Stated otherwise, guys need to maximize their wife's experience of their main emotional goal of security and safety before they can experience the maximization of admiration and physical expression by their wives, and vice versa. That is the whole point of *brag about*, e.g. *it is illegal for me to have one complaint about my spouse until I get them to the point of brag about*. That is the all-important work that leads up to the barrier reef gap between +5 and +6. Once there is a mutual feeling of *brag about* shared between both spouses, they can then be propelled over that reef into the beautiful waters of +6 to +10. Once that happens, it is easy for each spouse to say, "Whatever you want, you get, baby."

How Many Times per Week?

Among many other discoveries I have been fascinated by over my 30 years of working with couples is the consistency of responses to this question. First, let me be clear. I never ask the guy this question (hopefully it's obvious as to why). I ask wives, "If couples were healthy, how many times per week should there be intimacy?" The answer has been the same among 98% of wives that I have asked: "Two to three times per week." Amazing, almost every single time, the answer is the same. Now we get into what those two to three times per week look like. The easiest one to describe would be when you come together as couples after your date night. Men, we all know about "foreplay" and our wife's desire to be romantically pursued. If there is a noticeable gap of time in-between when wives aren't feeling pursued romantically by their husband and yet they are still asking them to "meet our needs," there is going to be trouble . . . and there should be. If we accomplish the three goals of date night (have fun, flirt, and show affection), and if we are great at scheduling the minimum, that feeling should never be present within our partners. However, we should still be pursuing the ever-coveted title of *brag about* by being consistent and regular at the actions of pursuit I described above.

So, what about the other times of the week? If the wife feels pursued by her husband, then she normally is completely okay with the other times being "quickies." However, in the session, I also get really personal with the couple and open up the topic of "what's permissible" because sometimes the couple has been way too shy to discuss it up until this point. I ask the wife if she is open to other sexual forms other than sexual intercourse, and most women are open to using their hand, oral sex, or talking sexually in her husband's ear while he pleasures himself. During these other experiences, I want to encourage the wives not to frame these other experiences through the lens of "feeling close" to their husbands. If everything I described above is happening, and there aren't any unresolved issues between the two of you (that should be resolved immediately), then frame these other experiences under "whatever you want you get." Please hang with me, ladies. Yes, I am a man, but I believe I am being objective here.

Allow me to expand the definition of pursuit. In addition to romantic acts of pursuit, what are other times when we feel pursued by our spouse? I believe it is when we are serving one another in a couple of unique ways. First, on a humorous note, when talking to couples about their pursuit of one another and the wife feels her man is falling short in this area, he naturally gets defensive and tries to convince her he is pursuing her. I would ask for specific examples, and he would actually, believe it or not, that he helped clean up after dinner. I then lovingly remind him of the definition of pursuit, and then slowly but surely, he is found wanting. To help bail him out, I validate his intention to serve but equip him with more effective ways to do it. When it comes to serving one another, and it truly feeling like pursuit, I point out the idea that there are normally specific chores that we take on as spouse's and are solely responsible for their completion, such as yard maintenance or laundry. If the husband came home one Friday afternoon and noticed the lawn was immaculate and he saw his wife outside working and sweating, he would definitely feel pursued. Likewise, if the wife came home and all the laundry was done (correctly, I might add) and put away, she would definitely feel pursued. The other way to pursue one another in service is to be a *servant*. This is when we do things for one another that is not a chore but a pure selfless act of love. If she gives him a thorough back rub, using oils, if he gets the lotion and gives her a foot rub, or if he draws a bath for her and puts on soft music and candles, each spouse respectively will absolutely feel pursued. The key common denominator with all of these is *proactive*. We obviously would never ask our spouse to do these things, and a major component of what makes these things so powerful is the surprise element of them.

What I am proposing, ladies, is that the same goes for sexual pursuit. Remember that the true feeling of significance and admiration is tied to the sexual experience of his wife. He wants to be admired and sexually desired. Many wives tell their husbands to let them know if they want something sexually, and for many men, that works. But think how powerful it would be if the wife approached her husband and said, "I want to do [this] to you tonight, would you like that?" Talk about your Thumper response! Even if men are okay with asking for a sexual experience, they still wants their wives to engage sexually in such a way as to fulfill admire/desires. At this point, I hear two common obstacles for wives to accomplish this: 1) she is not in the mood, or states that she doesn't have the same libido her husband has, or she would feel like she is compromising herself morally or in her purity, 2) she doesn't know how to do what I am describing and doesn't feel confident in herself and is resistant to do it. With the first obstacle, I ask wives to reframe it by seeing it as an act of love and meeting her husband's emotional needs and to avoid making her degree of libido or emotional desire a pre-requisite to doing it.

Question: when husbands rub your feet, do they first evaluate their desire to do so? Do they wait until they are in a loving mood? There are no emotional prerequisites when I decide to rub my wife's feet. I do it because she loves it. Should we be in the mood to show our spouse love? In life, there is what we should do and what we want to do. None of us wait for an emotional desire before we do what we should do. I don't feel like getting up to work out, to do the dishes, take out the trash, sit down with my children to do homework, or mow the lawn . . . I just do it because I should do it. When it comes to pursuing our spouses, we shouldn't wait until we *feel* like it. We should do it because it's the right thing to do if we are committed to loving our spouses. Second, and this is HUGE: we must not make the pursuit of our spouse contingent upon their pursuit of us. Biblically, I am supposed to love my wife as Christ loved the church, and when I stand before him, I won't be able to lay down the card that I didn't do it because I didn't feel pursued by my wife (which I absolutely do, by the way). Couples start the downward trend because of this very issue. Stop. Do you know what motivates me? My identity, value and worth is in my control (read my first book). I decide what I do, who I am, and how I am known by others. I am going to pursue my wife to the point, and consistently have, so she can say that she has never been loved like I love her. *I* want that testimony, and I want to walk out of this life having peace and confidence that this is who I am. I will not make my success in any area contingent upon other people. I suggest you do the same. Pursue your spouse in the ways you know you should pursue your spouse regardless of how you feel or whether you are motivated to do it. Classic disclaimer: if you are being treated poorly by your spouse, then this does not apply. I hate having to give no-brainer disclaimers, but there you go. This entire discussion assumes you are on the positive side of the number line as a couple.

Let's discuss the second obstacle that she doesn't know how to do what I am describing, doesn't feel confident in herself, or is resistant to do it. I confidently confront both men and women when they give this incredibly flimsy, and frankly selfish, excuse. If your child came to you and said they don't want to do their chores because they don't know how to do them, what will you say to them? If they want to play sports, but not practice their skills, what is your advice to them? LEARN. Guys, if you don't know how to give a great foot rub, learn how to do it. Back rubs? Same. Ladies, if you don't know how to verbally communicate that you admire and desire (sexually) your husband, learn how to do it. Yes, I am going to say it... the same goes for the sexual acts. Ladies, if you are philosophically okay with doing sexual acts other than intercourse, then learn how to do it. Please don't frame these things as "dirty" if you already said you are okay with doing them. You know they are not dirty, and if your husband is okay with doing the same to you, then there should be no hesitation on your side, either. Both spouses should become absolute skilled masters in every area of pursuit to our spouses. It is a skill, learn how to do it. If your spouse continues to give (B.S.) excuses why they can't, then let it go, and I'm sorry. Continuing to discuss it only creates anger and moves you further away from the goal. These things are very sensitive and rest on unstable ground. Too much movement will make it crumble. Just keep pursuing and ensuring your spouse is at *brag about* status and discuss it occasionally, when it comes up, but tread lightly. Another crucial point: my wife will never, ever ask me for a foot rub. Knowing this, I started *Foot rub Fridays* and try to give her a foot rub once a week! She loves it. Ladies, some husbands will ask, but if your husband is not asking, then he is like my wife. He will never, ever ask for sex or one of the other acts. This is most likely because it is far more about being admired and desired than it is the actual act. If husbands must constantly ask, they it feels obligatory, which is a complete turn-off. Imagine how crazy your man would go if you asked him, "May I do *this* to you tonight?"

Bait and Switch

Several husbands have lamented in couple's counseling about how much their wives have changed since marriage. I have heard countless stories from couples that, prior to marriage, they exhibited the level of passion found in the Song of Songs. Even though it should not happen (biblically), many spouses recount how sexual they were and how frequently they were engaging in sexual experiences with one another. After marriage, it seems to just die off. Why? Did the woman's libido leave the celebration of the marriage like the wedding guests? Many men feel like their wives pulled the "bait-and-switch" on them. They won their husbands to the altar by being everything sexually the guy wanted, but after the marriage, started to complain about low libido. Likewise, many women complain about the same thing. Men and women, these things should not be so. Marriage is hard work, and this section is exactly why. You both must work hard in pursuit and don't allow yourself the excuses anymore. Men, does she feel **captivated** by you? Why not? Is she not worth it? Did you lie at the altar? Are you angry because she is not meeting your needs? I understand, I truly do. Ladies, does he feel sexually admired and desired by you? Why not? Is he not worth it? Did you lie at the altar? Are you hurt because he is not meeting your needs? I understand, I truly do.

Both of you, I'll remind you what I stated earlier: You both want the other person to feel emotionally and relationally safe. As well, when you two are at your absolute best and are crushingly in love and would say, "This is us," THAT is who you truly are as a couple. Whenever you don't feel safe with one another or when you are angry and hurt, that is the *anomaly*, the fake, the foreign. Use communication skills, encourage one another, tell one another that you want to experience a +6 to +10 marriage, and start pursuing each other like crazy! You will be surprised how quickly you come out of the dark valley of this season!

CHAPTER 9:

I³ – Information, Interpretation, Intensity

My beloved put his hand by the latch of the door,

and my heart yearned for him.

– *Song of Songs 5:4*

Why would I wait until the very end to introduce the topic of the title of the book? The process of I³ is a simple, easy-to-memorize system that you can use to incorporate all the concepts of this book. I don't remember when I developed this tool, but it was at least 20 years ago. I have used it in my jobs as a pastor, professor, counselor, coach, and consultant. It became a ubiquitous tool because, everywhere I worked, I saw people living life according to false information, leading to enormous assumptions and narrowness in their thinking that severely lacked critical thinking. Their intense emotion shows they believe opposing views violate these principles and deserve swift justice, which they are eager to deliver. Once you master this process, you'll experience the same. Arguments will fall apart before your eyes. You will see holes in people's logic so large you'll feel compelled to lunge out to them and yell, "Look out!" to keep them from falling in. Sometimes, you'll stand there with an obviously stunned look on your face and the only words you can muster are, "Bless-your-heart." Let me lay out the paradigm of I^3, explain it, and then give multiple examples of how to apply it.

I liken the I^3 process to the engineering of the Panama Canal. The Panama Canal was created to greatly shorten the travel time it takes ships to go between the Pacific and Atlantic Oceans. It is located just north of South America in Panama, which is south of Costa Rica. It takes ships eight to ten hours to move through the Panama Canal, but if it wasn't available, it would take approximately 22 days for ships to travel around South America! It is one of the greatest engineering feats that humanity has ever accomplished. It is not like a river where ships just pass through, but a series of locks that fill up and drain to transition the ship from one side to the other. A ship would transition from either ocean into a lock that fills up with water to the height of the next lock, which then fills up with water to the height of the next lock, to the next lock, to the top, which is Gatùn Lake. Then, they do the same process on the way down, with each respective lock emptying its water to the level of the next lock. There are three locks that go up to Gatùn Lake, which is 85 feet above sea level, and three locks that go back down to the ocean. Each lock takes about 20-30 minutes to fill or empty. Use this same engineering concept when using the I^3 process.

Information-Interpretation-Intensity
Information
Formula Formation: *It is illegal for me to have any opinion and any emotion until I have all the information.*

Information is simply the story of the event. It is the topic, data, facts, and even assumptions used to formulate an opinion about what happened and what to do about it. Like the boats in the Panama Canal, you must wait until this first lock is as full as possible before you transition to the second lock, which is your interpretation of the information in the first lock.

He who answers a matter before he hears it, it is folly and shame to him. (Proverbs 18:13)[9]

To answer before listening—that is folly and shame (Proverbs 18:13)[10]

Soon after I re-committed my life to Christ, I fell in love with the book of Proverbs. There is inexhaustible wisdom within that book. Certain verses immediately stood out to me, probably because of the need for me to apply them! Proverbs 18:13 is certainly one. The reason why is that I had so many experiences getting upset about something, only to find out *there was more to the story*, and as soon as I heard the rest of the story, my opinions and emotions would immediately change. I then felt foolish for *jumping to conclusions* and regretted being so consumed with what I heard, and the negative assumptions I made about the person or situation weren't even true. When I then read these proverbs and heard God's conclusion that it was folly and shame, I immediately made it a major focus of mine to make sure I applied that in every situation I could. There was a theme I discovered when I struggled the most to apply this wisdom. It was when I *wanted what I heard to be true*. When I heard a story

---

[9] The Holy Bible, New King James Version, Copyright © 1982 Thomas Nelson
[10] Holy Bible, New International Version®, NIV® Copyright © 1973, 1978, 1984, 2011 by Biblica, Inc

or example that supported my beliefs and opinions, then I readily grabbed ahold of it and used that information myself, only to find out it wasn't true. This most often occurs when we hear something negative about someone we don't like, or who doesn't like us. The negative story supported and aligned with my beliefs about that person, so I just accepted it and didn't challenge it or gather more information like I should have.

The first one to plead his cause seems right, until his neighbor comes and examines him (Proverbs 18:17).[11]

If there was ever a time in human history where the wisdom of this verse needs to be applied, it is now. With all our technology and social media, which can be either good or evil, there is an addiction to "liking" and "sharing" posts that support your opinion. People are getting hurt and losing their lives from the complete lack of discipline in this area. From online bullying and hating to riots and physical attacks, this is serious. Thankfully, as societies around the globe are starting to suffer the ramifications, there is more discernment and caution being applied by many, but of course, there is no caution whatsoever among many more. We only have control over ourselves and can only influence so many people, but by the grace of God, please try and influence as many as you can to apply this truth. If you ever hear from someone the phrase, "I heard that . . .", then every bell and whistle in your mind should go off because you can assume you don't have all the information.

The mental model process starts with a story of he/she/they did/said. Your mental model (shaped by DNA, experiences,

---

[11] The Holy Bible, New King James Version, Copyright © 1982 Thomas Nelson

choices) acts like a computer, generating responses to your consciousness without judgment. It uses the information it has gathered since birth and the formulas you have trained it to use throughout your life. The effectiveness of your formulas is a direct product of your logic, reasoning abilities, and critical thinking. Your brain uses a formula to determine how much to engage before forming an opinion, and this formula needs constant adjustment for effectiveness. It's easy and natural to respond emotionally, as that's our instinctive reaction from birth. As our brain develops, we start adding logic and reason to our decision-making processes, but our emotional being isn't so easily tamed. A key concept in Dialectical Behavior Therapy (DBT) is called the Wise Mind Principle. The wise mind is the combination of both the emotional mind and the logical mind. Both are needed in any given scenario. Much of this book has discussed what happens if there is a void in responding to situations. Emotions are the driving force for us to solve problems and increase our quality of life, but without logic, the consequences of having the wrong amount of emotional energy could be dire. Our mental models offer quick suggestions, but because emotional energy often prioritizes self-interest, we need to pause and let our logical minds contribute. This process demonstrates emotional intelligence skills like impulse control and delayed gratification. By incorporating the formulas from this book, we can train our minds to engage more of our brains in auto-responses. Impulse control is the first emotional intelligence (EI) skill that we need to develop, and it is critical to our experience of negative emotions. Thankfully, it is very easy for us to recognize it when we have negative emotions, so that becomes the red flag for us to pause everything and first assess whether we have all the information. Those who neglect to control their impulses continue to suffer because the environment rules their emotional state. *Whoever has no rule over his own spirit, is like a city broken down, without walls* (Proverbs 25:28).[12]

We've all experienced receiving new information after hearing an initial story that completely changed our opinion and response. Before we can move on to the next lock, we must investigate the reasoning behind their words or behavior. Have you ever been upset with someone who had the right information on the facts of the story, but after they explained why they made the decision they did, it made sense to you, and your opinion changed? Of course, we all have. The information we need to gather before having our own opinion or emotion goes beyond just the external, surface components of the story; it also includes understanding their own mental models and validating before criticizing or judging. There is no way to gather every necessary fact and detail before responding, but we don't have control over that. We do have the control and the responsibility to gather the information we can, do our best to understand the logic and rationale for the decision-making, and assume the best of motives and intentions. Once this lock is filled, then the next lock in the canal opens: interpretation. *Fools find no pleasure in understanding but delight in airing their own opinions* (Proverbs 18:2).[13]

---

[12] The Holy Bible, New King James Version, Copyright © 1982 Thomas Nelson
[13] Holy Bible, New International Version®, NIV® Copyright © 1973, 1978, 1984, 2011 by Biblica, Inc

Interpretation

Formula Formation: *Is there any other way of looking at it?*
Once we have all possible information (i.e. we got the *whole* story), then we need to find a way to interrupt the next auto-response of our mental models, our interpretations, opinions, and conclusions of that information. In this step, I simply list three options to help you challenge your models. It is simply negative, neutral, and positive. We don't need any help creating the negative interpretation because that is often the automatic response, is what propels the entire need to use this process in the first place. Next, we need to practice critical thinking skills by looking at any situation from other angles and other points of view. I suggest neutral and positive interpretations because they are unemotional and logical. The only way to have negative emotions is because our conclusion is that there is a problem to be solved. But what creates the problem in the first place? Remember what created our negative emotions: unmet expectations and blocked goals. Have you ever challenged the legitimacy of your expectations? Have you ever looked back and realized that it was a good thing the paths you tried to take toward your emotional goals were blocked? In the last two questions, we just used both a neutral and a positive interpretation of the situation.

Asking yourself if there is any other way of looking at a situation allows you to pause and challenge your immediate conclusion. But how do you discover all the other ways of interpreting a situation? First, you begin debating yourself and your conclusions. You can put yourself in the place of others and ask, "If someone were to completely disagree with me in the way I'm looking at this, where would they be right?" The goal is to find ways to step out of our subjective selves and into the minds of those with different information and opinions. How would people who have no vested interest in meeting your expectations or achieving your goals view your situation? Where would they be right? What about those who disagree with your expectations and the ways you choose to meet your emotional goals? Where would they be right? We're not looking to eradicate your opinions, interpretations, or judgments; we want to obtain *all* the opinions, interpretations, and judgments that are true so we can know how to respond effectively to any situation. Remember, we all have blind spots, so proactively seek insights from others who have more accurate and effective mental models. But don't be discouraged—they need yours too.

Without consultation, plans are frustrated, but with many counselors they succeed (Proverbs 15:22).[14]

I also will reach back and pull in the concepts of rational, healthy, wise, and right (RHWR). Another way to both debate our original interpretations, as well as add new ways of thinking about our situation is to use the RHWR paradigm. Remember, we are all accountable for this paradigm, but we can also appeal to it. We hold ourselves accountable to it by asking, "Are any of my opinions irrational? Are they unhealthy? Unwise? Or just plain wrong?" Additionally, we can appeal to RHWR after we have filtered all our opinions through this paradigm, and once an opinion passes the test, we can hold on to it with all our might and allow it to guide our responses.

---

[14] New American Standard Bible, Copyright © 1960, 1971, 1977, 1995, 2020 by The Lockman Foundation, La Habra, Calif.

The last point I want to make for this section is to remind you of what I stated in the first chapter. Finding other ways to interpret the situation takes a lot of humility and work, but this is exactly what the Lord meant when He told us to cry aloud for knowledge, insight, wisdom, and understanding. Search for it like we would hidden treasure, *for then we would understand the fear of the Lord.* The fear of the Lord can mean very different things. For those who see Him as good, the fear of the Lord is centered in a humble understanding that there is so much we do not see or understand, but He does. We naturally think that when we fear something, we run from it, but because He is good, we run *to* Him. We fear Him because we are blind and need His insight for all things and are afraid that if we don't interpret any given situation correctly, it will have negative repercussions, causing pain to ourselves and others.

Intensity

The first two steps force us to hold back the immediate impulse reaction we had when an event in our environment sparked us. Our immediate impulse reaction, containing a powder keg of negative emotional energy, is produced from our mental model assuming the role of our over-stimulated, raging bodyguard who has only one job: eradicating any and all threats. We tell that bodyguard to heel to gather all the information we can that was not included in that first reaction. This information includes the chronology of events that led up to it, as well as the details surrounding the context of the situation, and finally the analysis of what the person was trying to achieve when they chose that action. All this information gathering will start forming other interpretations that either agree with, disagree with, or co-exist alongside of the immediate impulse opinion of the bodyguard. You keep asking yourself if there is any other way of looking at (interpreting) the information, you then list ALL the RHWR interpretations across the negative, neutral, and positive spectrum. You can tell that filling the second lock is an intense but powerful process because at this point you can compare the amount of negative emotional energy you are feeling at this moment, compared to the amount of emotional energy your enraged bodyguard (e.g. your mental model) had when the event that sparked the reaction first occurred.

At this point you then ask yourself what would be the most effective and RHWR response to that event. It may be to make a phone call, send a text, set up a meeting, or there may be several action steps. Whatever it is, that response will only take so much emotional energy (intensity). We then burn that emotional energy on the response and then it's over and we are at rest again. In real life, this is never the conclusion because every relationship and circumstance is like a tennis match and will be an ongoing exchange of responses. The I^3 process is not a one-and-done experience but is actually a ***mental model formula*** that you want to master in order to be successful at achieving the goal of the entire premise of both of my books: to remove all power and control the environment currently has over you. The goal is not to have zero emotional energy from the environment, but to have the right amount. It is RHWR for the environment to *influence* and *impact* us, but it is not RHWR for the environment to *control* our emotional energy.

The I³ process is a powerful, simple tool to use in the moment to ensure an emotionally intelligent response. However, even if you are successful in your mastery of the I³ technique, you will still need to address why the immediate impulse reaction your mental model was the enraged bodyguard, and why that bodyguard keeps showing up in situations that do not require that level of protection because the threat level in the situation does not warrant that level of protection. We now come full circle and find ourselves right back at the beginning of the first chapter of my first book. ***Every time our immediate impulse mental model response produces an amount of emotional energy that exceeds what is rational, healthy, wise, or right for that situation tells us, we need to go back to chapter one and walk through the process again.*** Don't be discouraged, you should know logically this process will need to be repeated over and over. However, each time it gets easier and takes less and less time to walk through. We will never perfect the process because each new season of our lives brings new people, new experiences, and reveals new things about ourselves we did not know were there. Welcome to life in all of its mystery and depth!

You can't impart what you don't possess. As I wrote this book, there was a great peace and confidence I felt, knowing that I have fully saturated my heart with all these principles, truths, and techniques. Actually, the entirety of these principles, truths, and techniques were the product of my own exposure, insecurities, pain, and wrestling with what I knew to be true and holding tightly to it as it pulled me through the most powerful periods of my life. I thank God for being so good, Jesus for being my First Love and

Fiancé, and the Holy Spirit for allowing me to taste and experience His signs, wonders, and miracles. I also thank my mentors, my friends, my seven kids and their spouses, and my wife, who is the absolute proof of the grace of God in my life.

The Power of I³:
What is the most emotionally intelligent RESPONSE?

INFORMATION (Data)
- Do I have all of the information?
- *It is illegal to have any opinion or any emotion until I have all of the information.*

      INTERPRETATION (-   N   +)
- Is there any other way of looking at it?
- *Wisdom means interpreting the situation through all truths.*

           INTENSITY (1----------------10)
- How much emotional energy is needed to respond to the situation?
- *What is being exposed in me?*

APPENDIX A:

RECOVERING FROM FAILURE

Sadly, a very common topic that propels a couple to start marriage counseling is when one partner chooses an immoral path to achieve their emotional goal. These immoral paths can be affairs, whether emotional or physical, pornography, or other sexual experiences like chat rooms. For this chapter, I will illustrate the healing process through the lens of a husband having a physical affair. But every one of these examples above have to do with giving our relational and/or sexual affection to someone other than our spouse. Both spouses can be guilty of this. As I wrote earlier in the book, men's sins are outward and offensive (sexual sins), and while some women do the same, many women need to be honest with themselves and ask if their relational affection that should be going to their husbands are being misdirected to other relationships in her life. It is not as offensive because it's not sexual, but it is still a form of unfaithfulness.

While the details are different couple to couple, there is certainly a "Groundhog Day" feeling I get every time I hear the story in the first session. Most of these mistakes occur from the felt vacuum of unmet needs in the marriage. However, I will say I have seen a significant number of occurrences happen not because of unmet needs, but simply from a lack of contentment. Their partner is meeting their needs, but the spouse *just wants more*. As soon as the couple is finished telling their story, I tell them that we are going to separate the offense from the marriage issues and deal with the offense first. The reason for this is the immediate fight that ensues when the offended party asks why the offense happened and the offender makes the mistake of saying their needs weren't being met. The offended party immediately strikes back and says, "Well my needs weren't being met either, but I didn't go out and screw somebody!" This is also true. Regardless of if there were unmet needs, there is absolutely no excuse for an affair. I tell them that we will absolutely address the issues in the marriage, but that is on hold until we establish the system and the process for how to heal from the offense.

I ask them to picture a rectangle standing on end with a diagonal line going from one corner at the top, down to the opposite corner, but not all the way, leaving a little space. On the side of the rectangle is the word TRUST. At the widest part at the top are the initials _WA, where the first letter is the offender's first initial. For example, for me, it would be GWA, which means Greg's Word Alone. Whenever there is complete trust, my wife will believe what I say. At the bottom, when trust has been lost, the little space between the diagonal line and the edge is still GWA, while the widest part on the other side of the diagonal line is FPA, which stands for Full Proof Accountability. When trust is lost, the response and need is full-proof accountability. The offended partner asks a million questions along with wanting measures put in place to control behaviors and to expose all actions. Because we don't live in an age of technology where the offended spouse can buy an invisible device that hovers over their spouse 24/7 to see everything they are doing, there is still the unfortunate need to have to rely on their partner's word, hence the little area of GWA.

In order to rebuild trust, I list three crucial elements. First, *no new occurrences*. Whatever the behavior, there must be a complete cessation of those behaviors. No more communication with the other person, no more pornography, chat rooms, etc. Many offenders make the mistake of only doing this first step. They keep saying, "I'm not talking to them anymore!" You have heard the phrase *time heals all wounds*, which I completely disagree with, but it is true that time does decrease intensity. To heal, there are other elements. Second, triggers *are reminders, not accusations*. In the days, weeks, and months that follow the discovery of the offense, the offended party will want and need to process, vent, cry, interrogate, and do it all over again, and again, and again. The offender must allow this process, owning the fact that they are the ones that caused it, and not get defensive because the offended party is not (truly) accusing them, even though there may be literal accusations like saying they don't believe the affair has ended or that they have stopped looking at pornography. It is all about the offended party needing to process and vent. It is hard, but it is necessary and must be allowed. Finally, and most importantly, trust and restoration can only happen when the offender *shows true repentance*. The rest of this chapter unpacks this process. Here is a diagram of what is looks like:

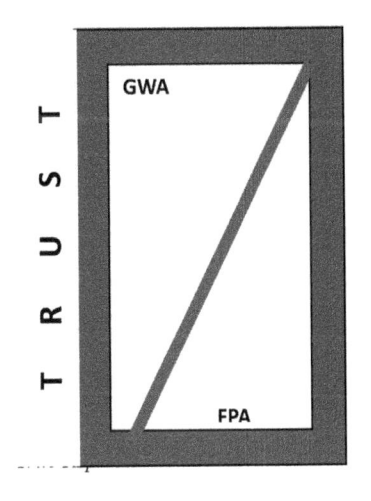

```
         GWA
T  ┌─────────┐
S  │        ╱│
   │       ╱ │      HOW TO REBUILD TRUST:
U  │      ╱  │
   │     ╱   │      1. NO NEW OCCURRENCES
R  │    ╱    │      2. TRIGGERS ARE REMINDERS, NOT
   │   ╱     │         ACCUSATIONS
T  │  ╱      │      3. SHOW TRUE REPENTANCE
   │ ╱       │
   └─────────┘
         FPA
```

True Repentance

Many times, when a couple comes in for the first session, the husband will be frustrated and say, "She hasn't forgiven me!" I then talk with the wife and ask her about forgiveness and what she understands forgiveness to be. After some discussion, I tell him, "She has forgiven you, but you need to understand that she is grieving." Husbands, or wives if they are the offenders, often don't frame the emotions of their spouses as *grieving*. The offended party is grieving the loss of the fidelity of their marriage, the loss of commitment, of being the only recipient of their partner's affection. The grieving process is shock, denial, anger, bargaining, depression, and acceptance. Where there is loss, I see the person cycle through the entire process several times, quickly, and then over time, the process slows down and the stages last longer. When the wife is in the anger phase, it may feel like she hasn't forgiven him. However, like with triggers, the husband must understand that forgiveness is her choice and may happen repeatedly throughout healing. Forgiveness doesn't mean 'moving on' emotionally; many think they haven't forgiven because they equate forgiveness with this ability. I teach that forgiveness is *making a choice to release the pursuit of and authority to judge, punish, condemn, seek revenge, or bring justice.* However, forgiveness is not forgetting, not waiting for an apology, not ceasing to feel pain, not a one-time event, not trusting, and not reconciliation. With this definition of forgiveness, the focus can turn to rebuilding trust and restoration.

In Christianity, forgiveness is a command, not an option. Matthew 6:15 states, "but if you do not forgive others their sins, your Father will not forgive your sins."[15] While forgiveness is commanded, choosing to rebuild trust and restore the relationship is 100% a freewill choice on behalf of the offended party. It is widely accepted that the offended party has every right to divorce, though many choose to try and rebuild trust and restore the marriage. That is why I separate the process of recovering from the offense from working on the marriage. The onus of responsibility is on the offender because the offended person is still deciding whether to continue in the marriage or call it quits. At this point, I walk the couple through the concepts of worldly sorrow and godly sorrow from 2 Corinthians 7. The Apostle Paul wrote the letter to the church reflecting on the experience he had with them when he confronted them about their sin and was grateful that they chose to respond with godly sorrow instead of worldly sorrow. Even though there is sorrow in both forms, there are key differences.

---

[15] Holy Bible, New International Version®, NIV® Copyright © 1973, 1978, 1984, 2011 by Biblica, Inc

I believe the main components of worldly sorrow are *guilt* and *shame*. These emotions are normal and acceptable, but the mistake is made when the offender's only focus and concern is the removal of these emotions. If this is the case, then the offended party just wants to move on and avoid the horrendous emotions. They feel if they have accomplished the cessation of the behavior, then they need to move on as a couple. The Apostle Paul says that worldly sorrow leads to death (separation). Relationally and emotionally, this makes complete sense because while it is understandable the husband feels guilt and shame, the focus and goal is absolutely not the alleviation of his negative emotions. If that is where the focus stays, there can be no rebuilding of trust and restoration.

Godly sorrow, on the other hand, leads to life and restoration. Thankfully, there is a very clear description of what this looks like in verse 11: "See what this godly sorrow has produced in you: what earnestness, what eagerness to clear yourselves, what indignation, what alarm, what longing, what concern, what readiness to see justice done. At every point, you have proved yourselves to be innocent [clear] in this matter."[16] When I read this verse out loud in front of the couple, I ask the wife, "Do you see these emotions and this level of response from your husband?" If you read over that verse a few times, even though there are no specific actions stated, you can easily observe that it is obvious whether the offender is responding in this way. You can't fake this response. I summarize this verse and say to the husband that if he was to truly embody godly sorrow, he would say something close to, "Honey, I can't

---

[16] Holy Bible, New International Version®, NIV® Copyright © 1973, 1978, 1984, 2011 by Biblica, Inc

stand what I did to you. I want to punch myself in the face for what I did. However, this is not about my emotions, it is about yours. I crushed your heart; I almost destroyed this marriage, and *I will do whatever it takes to make this right.*" That last phrase is a summary of verse 11. Using the trust paradigm above, then the first thing the husband needs to do is be proactive in creating a strategy for full-proof accountability. Does his wife have access to his computer, his phone, and can she always see his location? Regardless of the sexual sin, I advise that he install the program Covenant Eyes on all his devices. This safeguard has been around for a long time. The program takes a screenshot of the device every seven seconds or so, pixelates the images, and runs them through an AI program. Any inappropriate images are flagged. The husband needs to select someone to be their accountability partner and receive the daily email reports directly from Covenant Eyes. The husband needs to give permission to the accountability partner to immediately call his wife if the report shows he is looking at inappropriate material. I have found that most wives do not want to be the ones to receive the daily email because it is too much of a trigger, but the husband needs to discuss it with his wife; it's her decision. There may be other action steps the wife wants the husband to execute in order to fulfill FPA. If there is a disagreement, then they need to discuss it with their therapist. One of the most common points of disagreement is what to do if the affair happened with someone at work. Understandably, every time the husband goes to work, the wife worries all day, wondering what is happening. Many women want their husbands to quit and get a different job, but depending on the situation, the ramifications from that could be severe. If the husband owns the company, or is a partner, or is at a high enough level in the organization, quitting and getting a different job is extremely complicated. The principle of goal/path needs to be applied here. The goals are for the relationship to end, for communication to cease (if possible), and to set up an accountability structure to ensure that boundaries are set and adhered to. At the very least, the husband needs to find an accountability partner at work that is trustworthy and will actually hold him accountable. I suggest introducing the wife to the accountability partner, who should support the husband at work and update the wife on his progress. The goal is to heal the wife's heart, and if the husband is worried about his reputation, he should remember his actions. Each situation is unique, so approach this with care. There have been times when people are fired and there may even be legal ramifications for the company. It can be a real mess. Just remember goal/path and brainstorm ways to achieve the goals. In other situations, it is completely RHWR for the wife to demand the husband get a different job. It will take time, of course, but again if he is committed to do whatever it takes to make it right, he will go to great lengths to achieve this. Other things to consider to bring about change may be a rethinking of being a member of particular clubs, gyms, and even may need to end friendships because of the affair. It's painful, but it is all a part of the consequences of the mistake.

The steps to achieve FPA and to create boundaries still doesn't deal with the core issue. A husband naturally thinks that if the behavior or relationship ends (cessation of behavior) and they work on their marriage to ensure they're meeting needs, then that should be enough to heal from the process. But it's not, and his wife knows it's not. If either spouse has an affair or falls into an inappropriate relationship or other sexual sins, then it is mandatory to take a deeper journey to uncover what drove the person to commit these harmful behaviors. In my personal story, I had an emotional affair, but because I was a pastor and a counselor, I knew that I had to deal with my deeper issues. I go into length about this in my first book. What I will say here is that even though you may have been hurting from unmet needs in your marriage, it does not entitle you to look at pornography or have an affair. In addition to the negative emotions produced from unmet needs, there is a large quantity of negative emotions produced from insecurities, lies you believe, an underdeveloped identity, value, and worth, and/or very painful past experiences (trauma). This must be addressed because these are major drivers of the immoral behaviors.

In addition to suggesting the husband install Covenant Eyes on all his devices, I also assign the husband to go through the Journey Course (www.thejourneycourse.com). This is a very affordable online course led by Jay Stringer who is a therapist, a Christian, and someone who struggled with sexual addiction. It is a phenomenal course that takes a couple of months to complete. I explain to men that there are four components related to our sexual drive. The first is biological, namely testosterone. That one component is responsible for libido. No testosterone, no libido. The second one is related to our discipline and maturity, which is impulse control. The battle of the mind for the man begins at puberty and does not conclude until we take our last breath. We must train ourselves to control our minds and bodies and not give in to impulse. The maddening tension for young men is to understand and accept that this drive is what makes him pursue girls with the eventual goal of marriage and family. It's the very thing that ensures the survival of any species. However, this engine of desire can go from 1,000 to 5,000 RPMs within seconds. So, let's talk about the line between healthy attraction and lust. There has been an unending debate on where this line is. A man is just minding his business and going about his merry way, when he catches a glimpse of *her*. Guys are visually stimulated, and it happens so fast that it is impossible to control this, and we shouldn't. Noticing an attractive female is not a sin. God created beauty, and in our species, women are blessed with this, and men are left wanting. The testing comes in the immediate several seconds that follow. Some say that it's the second look that is lust, some say if you stare for more than three seconds it is lust. I don't understand the debate. Jesus said that lust is in the heart (Matthew 5:28) and every guy is different. My definition of lust is when you are sexually aroused by someone who is not your spouse. This applies whether you are single or married. You know whether you sinned or not. Impulse control is exercised right at this point. If men work hard and train themselves right at this moment, then the chances of them falling into sexual sin decrease greatly. As you might expect, wives become extremely sensitive and aware of their husband's eyes after the discovery of sexual sins. The danger is that she then takes on the role of the Holy Spirit and becomes his accountability partner in this area, and it doesn't go well. However, it is true that many husbands don't practice impulse control with their eyes and have developed a habit of scanning the immediate area and consistently resting their eyes on other females. I am okay with a wife pointing out that his eyes are wandering, and the husband needs to own the fact that if others observed him, they would agree his eyes wander too much. He needs to train himself to look where he is going, but he doesn't need to constantly look around. Guys, you need to understand how much it hurts our wives when we do this. It communicates to her that her beauty is not enough for you to be content. Stop it. While I say it is okay for the wife to point out that his eyes are wandering, it is *not* okay to accuse him of lusting because you don't know his heart ladies, and *you* need to also own the fact that you are sensitive and insecure right now (as you should be). But at the same time, you don't know what is going on in his heart, and these conversations will always increase the tension. Guys, if your wife voices her concern in any way, this is what you need to say: "Honey, all sin is confessed, and there is no foothold." Lust in the heart is an issue between the man and God. He needs to train himself in impulse control and keep a short account with the Lord by confessing and repenting immediately if he lusts. Ephesians 4:27 warns that failing to confess and repent allows sin to take root in the heart, becoming a stronghold that's increasingly difficult to break. Making this statement to your wife tells her you are keeping a short account with the Lord, and you haven't fallen into the sin again. Additionally, I strongly encourage a man to send his wife a daily text, right before bed, that reassures his love for her, that he is being pure, and that his heart is fully hers. It is okay to copy and paste every night because it communicates nothing is hidden and you have made it through the day being faithful to her in your heart. The next component is *admired and desired*. Testosterone creates libido, and guys must control this libido by training themselves in impulse control, but what is enmeshed with the sexual drive is a guy's emotional goal of significance: to be admired and desired sexually by his wife. We have already discussed this at length. The fourth component is *fantasy*. Every guy has a fantasy in his mind about the ultimate sexual experience, and every guy has his own unique wants and desires that make up this fantasy. This would be the *Thumper* ideas he would text his wife.

These four components are a part of every man's sexual experience. What the Journey Course points to and uncovers are all our life experiences that have inflated the intensity of these four components. Some are obvious, such as being exposed to pornography as a child or being molested, and some elements are not so obvious. I won't go into all these elements here because it is a deep and thorough process, and the Journey Course will walk him through it. These life experiences inflate the needs and the desires of the man to the point that the degree of his needs and desires don't pass the RHWR test. This dynamic is dangerous, as the wife's inability to meet these desires leaves the husband trapped in unfulfilled expectations, fueling frustration and anger. Over time, this anger breeds entitlement, driving him to justify immoral choices to satisfy his physical and emotional needs. I have walked many men through this process and coached them through the Journey Course and it is a very powerful, healing process. Part of the process is for the man to write *My Journey Story,* where he lists all the life experiences that led to the inflation of his desires, describes his sexual sins and how it was discovered, and finally writes how he has healed by addressing his insecurities related to his identity, value, and worth and trauma.

True repentance drives the husband to actively pursue FPA and approach his wife with acceptance and openness, willingly discussing the offense and its impact whenever she needs to process it. This addresses the second element of how to rebuild trust. Reflecting back on 2 Corinthians 7:11, the husband exhibits that he is absolutely crushed and devastated for what he has done to his wife, so much so that the wife begins to be concerned about the state of his pain. Simultaneously, he begins an intense pursuit to win her heart back. She needs to feel that he is absolutely captivated by her. I tell the husband that *she will begin to heal when she feels he is pursuing her harder than he has pursued anything else.* Many husbands downplay how much he cared for the other woman, but it doesn't matter. He will never convince his wife of this. It is completely a matter of her experience of his affection and pursuit. That is why I use the word *captivated*. There is a level of intensity of pursuit at that level that if a wife were to use that word, he is doing what he needs to do. The marriage needs to be completely different than it was before the affair occurred, or else the wife will continue to worry that the husband is still experiencing the same level of discontentment.

Once this description is given and implemented, I then begin working with the couple on their marriage, using the approach in this book. If the husband has a 2 Corinthians 7:11 response for a long enough period time, and they are implementing the tools in this book, then healing will start to take place. There are various theories about how long this process should take, but it is really up to the couple. I don't like putting a time on it because time is not the goal; it is the transformation of the marriage. The last component of the restoration process is the final phrase in verse 11: being innocent and clear in this matter. Full restoration and being innocent and clear means that the ledger is clear, the topic has concluded, and this chapter has closed. When the wife continues to struggle beyond this point, then the situation is exposing something deeper in her. If the husband senses this struggle, he can ask, "Is there anything else I can do to make this right? Have I done everything I can to make this right?" If the answer is yes, then the wife needs to release the offense and allow it to be closed. If she can't, then the focus needs to turn from the hurt from the offense to the deeper issues that may be in her heart, such as her identity, value, and worth, and healing from trauma that may have occurred earlier in her life. If this is the case, she needs to seek counseling individually to work through these things. The entire premise of my first I^3 book, and this one, is to encourage everyone to face the items in our hearts that we need to face. The doorway to these deeper truths is through our negative emotions.

APPENDIX B:

PARENTING

I include this section because it addresses a key aspect of our marriage and its core identity. To begin, I drew from my first book, where I applied objective truth to the goal of parenting.

Equipping: Using the Concept of Objective Truth in Parenting

To illustrate the contrast between the subjective and objective view of self, allow me to use an illustration from marriage counseling and parenting. As parents, we strive to raise great kids, and as all parents know, it is sometimes a very arduous process. Why is it sometimes so difficult? The degree of difficulty is directly correlated to how much our child disagrees with our opinion of where they need to grow, right? Why would they disagree with us? Well, from infancy, we are born with a tenacious drive to improve our quality of life using the path of our choice to achieve that goal. This process continues throughout childhood and into our teenage years. We try to coach our children to understand the difference between their subjective view of themselves to more of an objective view. It's a never-ending process of helping our young ones evaluate their paths through the objective RHWR grid (or some form of it). Our children, like us, fight against the application of this grid because all of us are committed to what we *want* to do.

As our children develop the ability to objectively assess us—flawed humans still growing—their resistance to objective RHWR naturally increases. It's human nature to evaluate the evaluator.

You may have heard the saying, "You can't separate the message from the messenger." When someone suggests change, we instinctively scan for hypocrisy. With children, this manifests in three ways: they question our slow progress toward their vision of our point B, get frustrated when we disagree on that vision, and lose respect if we're blind to our flaws, apply double standards, or lack urgency to change. To guide them from subjective to objective thinking, we must model accountability and uphold strong moral principles. But additionally, we need to be humble, own our mistakes, and show them how to recover from failure because we know it is easy for our children to feel like they are constantly failing. Conversely, lacking humility discredits us, and we lose their respect. Show them how to be teachable and teach them how to fail, as well as how to recover and grow. Show them how to achieve both goals of grace and truth with yourselves and with them. If we want them to be accountable to objective truth (RHWR), then we need to model it for them. Our children need to feel that we are not forcing them into a mold of our own making. I encourage parents to show their children that the goals for our parenting are objective and ubiquitous (present for everyone). Successful parenting is defined by our children becoming independent, successful, mature adults. Say to them,

"I am not imposing my ideals and values on you; my goal is to equip you and coach you to become an independent, successful, mature adult. Think of it like this: on one end is the 25-year-old (child's name) who is independent, successful, and mature, and on the other end is you at your current age. There is a gap between you right now and you at 25. This is not a conversation between you and me, but between the present-day you and you as an independent, successful, mature adult. When you are 25, you will look back at your current age and have the *exact same advice* that I am giving to you right now. I love you, and I want to equip and coach you to become that person." In addition, I would say, "Where I am selfish in this process is I am doing everything I can to make sure your future college roommate and spouse don't disparage me over the fact that they are having to deal with your lack of independence, lack of success, and immaturity, so let's keep working."

Kids need their parents to invest in and coach them to help them become the best version of themselves. Parental coaching does not shy away from correction, realizes the power of encouragement, and continually equips them for the real world. The countless number of parents to whom I have presented this mindset feel a great sense of relief because it eliminates the "fight" that the child perceives as parents imposing their own "opinions" on them. Like RHWR, there is objective truth among all humanity when we say that our children should be independent, successful, and mature. Every parent everywhere, at any point in history, agrees with that. Applying this process is rhetorical, it is common sense, it's ubiquitous, it transcends all cultures, all nations, all times…to train our children to be independent, successful, and mature. Objective truth hovers above us all, and our individual point B's and paths don't only impact us personally but also the lives of others. There must be rules, boundaries and standards by which all humans align themselves, despite any frustration it may cause as it may appear to block their main emotional goal of individuality and autonomy.

It is also important to teach our children to incorporate objective values, such as selflessness. Children don't naturally recognize the long-term effects of their obsession with individuality and autonomy. Pursuing these emotional goals creates the greatest emotional reward for them, but if this process becomes cemented, they will be extremely weak in their EI skills like impulse control and delayed gratification. This can absolutely ruin their chances of success in life and relationships. Another principle I give to parents, in addition to raising our children to be independent, successful, and mature, is the principle of "duty and discipline before dopamine." As adults, we do this every single day. Any independent, successful, and mature adult practices this principle. We work before we play. We do our household responsibilities before we relax. We eat vegetables before ice cream. It's standard, or it should be. Adults come to me for counseling, wanting to be better equipped to apply this principle. Many adults struggle with low impulse control and poor RHWR choices because their parents emphasized grace and empathy over truth and boundaries, leading to enablement. To give our children hope for personal and relational success, we must teach them to balance these principles. The resistance we may experience from our children is understandably rooted in their quest of the reward and immediate emotional goal being met. Yet their shortsightedness prevents them from seeing the future unintended consequences of either choosing their immediate emotional goals or non-RHWR paths.

Family Expectations Contract

I developed this tool while I was working at the Residential Treatment Center. When the teen patient was getting close to discharge, the parents (and the teen) had a lot of anxiety about what it would be like when their child came home after being at the RTC for weeks, even months. As we've discussed, our negative emotions comes from unfulfilled expectations. But the problem is these expectations were never evaluated, quantified, discussed, and agreed upon. We just experience a negative emotion, and immediately start burning negative energy trying to force everyone around us to change and meet that expectation.

Earlier in the book, I discussed applying this concept to marriage; here, I aim to help parents apply it to parenting. In final RTC family counseling sessions, we focus on setting clear, specific expectations so parents and teens share a clear vision of success. For instance, parents will say that they expect the teen to keep their room clean, and it's easy for the teen to agree. The problem: there are two very different expectations on the meaning of "clean", and very different definitions of the word "keep." It's a wonderful recipe for disaster. Another example the expectation that the teen gets good grades, gets their homework, and has a good attitude. Again, there is absolutely no problem getting agreement from the teen on these expectations, but there are very different interpretations of what success looks like, and more clearly, what lack of success looks like.

The most effective thing to do is be as clear and specific as possible in these expectations. What is far more crucial is to create clear, specific details on what the consequences are if the expectations are not met. At the end of this chapter is a sample contract I give to families to use. Each family must customize it to their specific family. Once you complete the kids' expectations, set up a family meeting to review the contract. Below the section on the expectations for the children, there is a section on expectations for parents. I'll go into detail later this, but this is for the children to fill out (final say by parents). Once completed, every member of the family signs the contract stating they understand it and will abide by any consequences should they not fulfill their duties. This process solves the recurring fights between parents and children about whether the child actually fulfilled the expectation, the severity and inconsistency of the consequence, and the hurt and anger caused by both the parent and the child.

At the top of the contract, I do list principles that apply to every family. These are:

Principle #1: To train and equip our children to be independent, autonomous, mature, and effective adults. (Described above)

Principle #2: Mastering impulse control and "Duty/discipline before dopamine." I discussed impulse control several times, and even referred to this principle above, but allow me to elaborate. Every adult must master some element of impulse control. However, there are still several adults who still struggle with impulse control in the areas of self-improvement (like exercising regularly) or even around technology. We want our children to be as successful as possible, and this principle is one of the, if not the, most important. As early as appropriate, start instilling this principle into your children in the areas of homework and chores. When they come home from school, they grab a snack, use the restroom, and relax a bit, which is fine, of course, but at some point, they come to a fork in the road. Do they get their homework done or do they watch TV, play on their phone, play video games, etc.? Include this expectation in the contract. The same applies to daily/weekly chores.

Principle #3: Master consistency in parenting. There are parents that are too soft and parents that are too strict. The most damaging style is inconsistent parenting. Since the day of birth, our children don't have a clue how to do this "life" thing, don't know how to respond to a variety of situations, and don't know how to evaluate the importance of each situation. As parents, we display different degrees of intensity and respond differently to the same situation. So, which is it, Mom and Dad? Is it the end of the world if they forget their lunch, or is it no big deal and you'll bring it to them? Should they be grounded for a month from their phone when they didn't take out the trash, or just reminded? Is it okay to ground them for a month, and renege on it and give them their phone back after a couple of days? Crazy, right? Our inconsistency needs to stop and the inconsistent responses between mom and dad equally need to stop.

Principle #4: Create a way for the child to be able to be restored and make it right. If the child receives a consequence that takes away a privilege, then offer a way for them to be restored and get it back by adding a chore (if the privilege is an activity that is occurring soon), or by educating themselves on the core issue by reading a book, doing research, and writing a report.

The next section of the contract is a table that lists the specific expectations on the left and the specific consequences or rewards on the right. The first one listed is on the topic of grades:

EXPECTATIONS	CONSEQUENCE/REWARD
KIDS' EXPECTATIONS	
Get A's and B's on all assignments.	Reward: If all "A's" & "B's" on their report card, then (child) will receive $50. Reward: If all "A's" on report card, then (child) gets $200. Consequence: If any grade for an assignment or test or quiz comes in below a "B", then no electronics until the next grade in the class is an "A" or "B".

Each child's academic expectations should align with their abilities. List each child's name and expectations in the left column, and use the right column for rewards and consequences, specifying what they must achieve to earn the reward. Instead of rewarding grades, we taught our children to strive for excellence by offering money for reading approved books and writing reports, reinforcing valuable principles. Grade-related consequences should align with the idea of prioritizing duty and discipline over instant gratification.

Don't wait until the end of the marking period. With current technology, we can track grades daily, allowing for immediate consequences and quicker restoration.

Next is chores. This, too, aligns with the principle of duty and discipline before dopamine. Like everything else, specificity is the key here. Further, considering Principle #1, I personally disagree with giving our children an allowance for doing things they *should* do as a member of the family. If they want to earn spending money, I suggest using the same theory as the reward in grades. Give them a task that is not their responsibility and over and above their list of chores. If they clean the refrigerator, weed the landscaping, pick up the dog poop in the backyard (we did this one), or anything else you can find, they can earn the amount of money you offer. Another possible reward is listed in the contract:

Daily chores completed immediately after homework completed **Weekly chores completed by noon on Saturday** **(List of chores on back)**	**Consequence:** If chore is not completed on time or to standard of parent, the child must immediately complete the chore, and a "deep clean" chore will be added (such as cleaning the toilet, the bathtub, the sink) and must be completed immediately after the first chore. **Reward:** If child succeeds by being independent and completes all chores without needing to be reminded for one week, then parent will take child to the restaurant of her choice (or a store to buy something - $10 limit).

List daily and weekly chores for each child, being as specific as possible. For tasks like cleaning, add "to the standard of the parent" to avoid disputes, and include clear deadlines for completion.

One more thing, Mom and Dad. Immediately, and I mean immediately, get out of the habit of reminding the child to do their chores. Remember, the goal is to coach them to be independent, autonomous, successful, and mature. The contract's strengths lie in the specificity of the expectations, including the deadline. They have all the skills and resources they need to accomplish this. If they don't, it is a matter of them choosing to not master duty/discipline before dopamine. Don't remind them, and once the deadline passes, initiate the consequence. Remember, they already signed the contract, stating they agreed to the expectations and the consequences. It is up to them to fulfill the expectations because that is what they will need to do as adults.

The next row or two are used to add expectations that are needed because the children developed a bad habit, and it needs to be "coached" out of them. Here are some examples:

Be respectful (as measured by parents) when asked to complete a task not in list of chores.	Consequence: Must immediately obey and will be assigned another task.
Independence and autonomy in tasks.	Consequence: If child has the capability and responsibility of doing the task, but asks someone else to do it because of laziness, child must immediately do the task and then serve another member of the family by doing a task for them.

Be at bus stop by 7:00 am	Consequence: If bus driver and students need to wait for child, child will write a letter of apology to bus driver and students that is to be read the next school day when child boards the bus.
No swearing (verbally or text)	Consequence: Child is to write a letter of apology to recipient of swear word. Letter is to include apology to person for disrespecting them, description of understanding that swearing is inappropriate, immature, and displays a lack of intelligence in word choice, and promise to honor the person and God in the future.
No lying	Consequence: In light of the degree of character weakness, the child will be assigned the duty of cleaning every toilet in the house. Or the child may choose to clean the master shower with a scrub brush.

Whatever is the habit, make sure the expectation is clear and that the consequence is weighty enough to make the child dread it. Some habits are personality weaknesses, lack of impulse control, or mild in nature; while others are much weightier, and, if left unchecked, will ruin relationships and have severe consequences. You want to weed those out ASAP!

The next few rows are situationally based principles and techniques, and if implemented, are very effective and protects you as parents from common parenting mistakes. These are:

Equip/Empower or Enable?	If the child wants something out of the blue (to do something or buy them something), ask yourself and/or your spouse, "If I/we did this for them or bought this for them, would I/we be a gracious parent, or would I be enabling them?" If enabling, then the answer is no. Or if the child misbehaves, ask, "If I/we just verbally corrected them and didn't give them a consequence, would I/we be a gracious parent, or would I be enabling them?" If enable, do "Delay of Sentencing" below.
Delay of Sentencing	If they do something that is inappropriate, disobedient, disrespectful, etc. then Mom and Dad will simply say, "There will be a consequence for what you did/didn't do," and then will discuss the appropriate consequence together and will communicate the consequence at some indetermined point in the future (no statute of limitations).
1-2-3	If Mom or Dad asks the child to do something (like pick up the living room), they will be asked, and then if the child delays in doing the task, the next statement will be, "This is #2, if I have to ask again, there will be a consequence." If there is still no response, the task must be done immediately, with another chore added to it, to be done immediately.

I believe the "Equip/Empower or Enable?" technique is self-explanatory. The next one, "Delay of Sentencing" will need some explanation. The name of this technique comes from how our justice system works. While there are several weaknesses to our system, there are two aspects I believe are very wise. First, there is a delay of a declaration of guilt, which is our motto of "innocent until proven guilty." In parenting, most of the infractions are clear, and there isn't any question of guilt, but there are situations where we will do well to take time to gather all the facts before assigning guilt. The second is after a person is declared guilty, there is normally a delay in sentencing so the judge can weigh all the facts, assess the egregiousness of the crime, and give out the appropriate sentence. We need to practice the same wisdom at home. When our child does something wrong that isn't in the contract, all you need to say is, "There is going to be a consequence for what you did." This is so effective in several ways. First, when we impulsively hand out a consequence to the child, what does the child think about from that point on? Right, the consequence. When we use this technique, the child will ask about the consequences, but we tell them we will think about it and let them know. Now what is the child processing? They are processing exactly what we want them to: what they did. They are weighing out what they did, the severity of it, why they did it, etc. Second, using this technique protects us from impulsively giving them a consequence that isn't well thought out, probably too extreme (or not extreme enough) and has nothing to do with the actual infraction. Nowadays, our default consequence is to ground the child from their phone. If a child disrespects us verbally, how does grounding them from the phone coach them at all? We need to be more intentional and strategic in what consequences we choose. The goal isn't just to cause suffering but to coach them as well and make it stick. Finally, it allows us to join forces with our spouse, tap into one another's strengths in deciding what the consequence should be, and because we both strategized, we show the strength of unity to our children.

When I share this technique with parents, I always relish the personal example I give them (my daughter hates it, but she doesn't have to know, does she). My wife and I have seven children between the two of us. Don't worry, there was only one left at home to raise when we got married. Thankfully, we didn't have to recreate the Brady Bunch. All our children are wonderful, and we are proud of every one of them. The same goes for our youngest. She is an absolute sweetheart, and I adore her beyond words. Although close, she has not quite obtained perfection. When she was a teen, we made the mistake of allowing her to watch a movie we shouldn't have allowed her to watch. To be transparent, it was the movie *Hangover*. Don't you dare judge, we aren't perfect either, and I said we made a mistake! A year or so after she watched that movie, she had one of her best friends spend the night and she asked in front of her friend, "Can we watch *Hangover* tonight?? C'mon, I have already seen it!" Excellent logic. We gave the standard response of, "Well, Amy (not her real name) hasn't, so text your mom Amy, and if she says it's okay, then yes, you can watch it." After that, my wife and I settled in our bedroom to watch TV, and about 20 minutes later, I "just had a feeling," so I got up and walked into our entertainment room to find the girls were 17 minutes into the movie. I looked over at Amy and asked, "Amy, did your mom give you permission to watch the movie?" She was only about eight feet from me, and as if I were a ghost, I got no response. Not verbal nor visual. She didn't acknowledge me, turn her head, nothing, she just kept watching the movie. I laughed and said again, "Amy! Did your mom give you permission to watch the movie?" Still nothing. Ok, that's it. I paused the movie and kneeled right in front of her and asked her again. At this point, our daughter piped up and said (again), "I've already seen the movie, it's fine!" I asked one more time, and finally, they admitted that they had texted her and she just hadn't replied yet. I turned to my daughter and said, "There is going to be a consequence for what you did." It turns out that Amy's mom absolutely did not want her watching that movie.

I returned to the bedroom and told my wife the story. It was actually funny because these girls are so sweet, and we just laughed at the fact that Amy did not even turn her head to answer me! We decided to come up with three consequences, and we would let our daughter decide which one she wanted. The first was to text Amy's mom, explain what happened, and apologize to her. The second was to write a certain number of sentences on what she did, and the third was to memorize Proverbs 14:2, which states, "Whoever fears the Lord walks uprightly, but those who despise him are devious in their ways."[17] She chose the third option. All of this happened on a Friday night, and on Sunday after church, I said to our daughter, "You haven't quoted the verse to me yet, so if you don't quote it to me by 6:00 p.m. tonight, I am going to add another one of the consequences of my choosing." She quoted it to me by the deadline.

When you give yourselves time to discuss it, you can think through exactly what the infraction is. Is it a lack of maturity? Or is it a bad attitude, or weak impulse control, or irresponsibility?

---

[17] Holy Bible, New International Version®, NIV® Copyright © 1973, 1978, 1984, 2011 by Biblica, Inc

The key is to not just give a punishment but to teach and coach the child in the very area where they made the poor choice. Our daughter was being sneaky, as well as devious in how she went about it. Additionally, when you allow the time, you can be very creative in the ideas of the discipline. I suggest doing what we did and giving them a choice among three options, so they are the ones choosing the consequence. You also can add one if they don't follow through with the first, but let the situation be your guide. Finally, there is no deadline for you to hand out the consequences. Sometimes, it is good to wait to let your child really sit and process what they did, or it is good to wait because they are hoping and assuming you forgot about it and are shocked when you give them the consequence a week after the infraction. Again, let the situation be your guide!

The final technique, 1-2-3, is for tasks that need to be done that aren't regular chores, like picking up the living room after watching a movie or something. There are two main goals this technique accomplishes, 1) immediate obedience by the child, and 2) keep you from escalating your frustration and anger after the 27th reminder to your child. This technique is very powerful if used regularly and maintains a peaceful and harmonious environment. However, be warned: the *only* way for this technique to work is if you are consistent with it. The same is true for the entire contract. Parents, please quit being so flighty in your parenting, blaming and excusing yourselves because "you're so busy." If you are, that is your issue to solve because you are not understanding the ramifications of your inconsistency. On the other hand, give yourselves grace. It takes time to mold the family culture to a contract like this but keep at it. The contract will need to be revised with each season because schedules change. Your child may grow out of their current weakness but will most certainly find another bad habit. Just keep working the plan, you'll be thankful you did!

The final part of the contract is for parents' expectations, allowing children to provide feedback on frustrating parenting habits. This is an opportunity to acknowledge your humanity and commitment to growth. When we form bad habits, we need to accept the fact that we need training and accountability to break these bad habits. You then ask them for some ideas on what they would love for you to change about yourself. For example, when working with a mom and a daughter, the daughter said, "I have told you that I get so mad every time I am explaining my side of the story, and you roll your eyes! You have promised not to do that, but you still do it!" The mom agreed, so that became the expectation. Let your children suggest consequences, but reserve final approval to ensure fairness. For example, you might give the affected child a dollar or take them to their favorite fast-food restaurant for each slip-up.

Both the mom and the dad must agree on the one expectation for the contract and an agreed upon consequence. As you revise the contract each season, your piece gets revised as well. Adding a parent's expectations section has so many benefits. It is done after you have explained the new system, so it makes your children much more accepting of the contract, and in some cases excited, because they can't wait for you to blow it and take them out to eat. It models for them that everyone needs to grow, everyone needs to be teachable, own their weaknesses, and be willing to be held accountable for their actions. After you complete this section, the parents edit the contract on their computer, print it, and everyone signs it, dates it, and displays it somewhere in a public area of the house. Here is what the contract looks like in full:[18]

I believe the "Equip/Empower or Enable?" technique is self-explanatory. The next one, "Delay of Sentencing" will need some explanation. The name of this technique comes from how our justice system works. While there are several weaknesses to our system, there are two aspects I believe are very wise. First, there is a delay of a declaration of guilt, which is our motto of "innocent until proven guilty." In parenting, most of the infractions are clear, and there isn't any question of guilt, but there are situations where we will do well to take time to gather all the facts before assigning guilt. The second is after a person is declared guilty, there is normally a delay in sentencing so the judge can weigh all the facts, assess the egregiousness of the crime, and give out the appropriate sentence. We need to practice the same wisdom at home. When our child does something wrong that isn't in the contract, all you need to say is, "There is going to be a consequence for what you did." This is so effective in several ways. First, when we impulsively hand out a consequence to the child, what does the child think about from that point on? Right, the consequence. When we use this technique, the child will ask about the consequences, but we tell them we will think about it and let them know. Now what is the child processing? They are processing exactly what we want them to: what they did. They are weighing out what they did, the

---

[18] You can go to https://www.becomingmore.com/resources-and-forms and find a downloadable contract.

severity of it, why they did it, etc. Second, using this technique protects us from impulsively giving them a consequence that isn't well thought out, probably too extreme (or not extreme enough) and has nothing to do with the actual infraction. Nowadays, our default consequence is to ground the child from their phone. If a child disrespects us verbally, how does grounding them from the phone coach them at all? We need to be more intentional and strategic in what consequences we choose. The goal isn't just to cause suffering but to coach them as well and make it stick. Finally, it allows us to join forces with our spouse, tap into one another's strengths in deciding what the consequence should be, and because we both strategized, we show the strength of unity to our children.

When I share this technique with parents, I always relish the personal example I give them (my daughter hates it, but she doesn't have to know, does she). My wife and I have seven children between the two of us. Don't worry, there was only one left at home to raise when we got married. Thankfully, we didn't have to recreate the Brady Bunch. All our children are wonderful, and we are proud of every one of them. The same goes for our youngest. She is an absolute sweetheart, and I adore her beyond words. Although close, she has not quite obtained perfection. When she was a teen, we made the mistake of allowing her to watch a movie we shouldn't have allowed her to watch. To be transparent, it was the movie *Hangover*. Don't you dare judge, we aren't perfect either, and I said we made a mistake! A year or so after she watched that movie, she had one of her best friends spend the night and she asked in front of her friend, "Can we watch *Hangover* tonight?? C'mon,

I have already seen it!" Excellent logic. We gave the standard response of, "Well, Amy (not her real name) hasn't, so text your mom Amy, and if she says it's okay, then yes, you can watch it." After that, my wife and I settled in our bedroom to watch TV, and about 20 minutes later, I "just had a feeling," so I got up and walked into our entertainment room to find the girls were 17 minutes into the movie. I looked over at Amy and asked, "Amy, did your mom give you permission to watch the movie?" She was only about eight feet from me, and as if I were a ghost, I got no response. Not verbal nor visual. She didn't acknowledge me, turn her head, nothing, she just kept watching the movie. I laughed and said again, "Amy! Did your mom give you permission to watch the movie?" Still nothing. Ok, that's it. I paused the movie and kneeled right in front of her and asked her again. At this point, our daughter piped up and said (again), "I've already seen the movie, it's fine!" I asked one more time, and finally, they admitted that they had texted her and she just hadn't replied yet. I turned to my daughter and said, "There is going to be a consequence for what you did." It turns out that Amy's mom absolutely did not want her watching that movie.

I returned to the bedroom and told my wife the story. It was actually funny because these girls are so sweet, and we just laughed at the fact that Amy did not even turn her head to answer me! We decided to come up with three consequences, and we would let our daughter decide which one she wanted. The first was to text Amy's mom, explain what happened, and apologize to her. The second was to write a certain number of sentences on what she did, and the third was to memorize Proverbs 14:2, which states,

"Whoever fears the Lord walks uprightly, but those who despise him are devious in their ways."[19] She chose the third option. All of this happened on a Friday night, and on Sunday after church, I said to our daughter, "You haven't quoted the verse to me yet, so if you don't quote it to me by 6:00 p.m. tonight, I am going to add another one of the consequences of my choosing." She quoted it to me by the deadline.

When you give yourselves time to discuss it, you can think through exactly what the infraction is. Is it a lack of maturity? Or is it a bad attitude, or weak impulse control, or irresponsibility? The key is to not just give a punishment but to teach and coach the child in the very area where they made the poor choice. Our daughter was being sneaky, as well as devious in how she went about it. Additionally, when you allow the time, you can be very creative in the ideas of the discipline. I suggest doing what we did and giving them a choice among three options, so they are the ones choosing the consequence. You also can add one if they don't follow through with the first, but let the situation be your guide. Finally, there is no deadline for you to hand out the consequences. Sometimes, it is good to wait to let your child really sit and process what they did, or it is good to wait because they are hoping and assuming you forgot about it and are shocked when you give them the consequence a week after the infraction. Again, let the situation be your guide!

The final technique, 1-2-3, is for tasks that need to be done that aren't regular chores, like picking up the living room after

---

[19] Holy Bible, New International Version®, NIV® Copyright © 1973, 1978, 1984, 2011 by Biblica, Inc

watching a movie or something. There are two main goals this technique accomplishes, 1) immediate obedience by the child, and 2) keep you from escalating your frustration and anger after the 27th reminder to your child. This technique is very powerful if used regularly and maintains a peaceful and harmonious environment. However, be warned: the *only* way for this technique to work is if you are consistent with it. The same is true for the entire contract. Parents, please quit being so flighty in your parenting, blaming and excusing yourselves because "you're so busy." If you are, that is your issue to solve because you are not understanding the ramifications of your inconsistency. On the other hand, give yourselves grace. It takes time to mold the family culture to a contract like this but keep at it. The contract will need to be revised with each season because schedules change. Your child may grow out of their current weakness but will most certainly find another bad habit. Just keep working the plan, you'll be thankful you did!

The final part of the contract is for parents' expectations, allowing children to provide feedback on frustrating parenting habits. This is an opportunity to acknowledge your humanity and commitment to growth. When we form bad habits, we need to accept the fact that we need training and accountability to break these bad habits. You then ask them for some ideas on what they would love for you to change about yourself. For example, when working with a mom and a daughter, the daughter said, "I have told you that I get so mad every time I am explaining my side of the story, and you roll your eyes! You have promised not to do that, but you still do it!" The mom agreed, so that became the expectation. Let your children suggest consequences, but reserve final approval to ensure fairness. For example, you might give the affected child a dollar or take them to their favorite fast-food restaurant for each slip-up.

Both the mom and the dad must agree on the one expectation for the contract and an agreed upon consequence. As you revise the contract each season, your piece gets revised as well. Adding a parent's expectations section has so many benefits. It is done after you have explained the new system, so it makes your children much more accepting of the contract, and in some cases excited, because they can't wait for you to blow it and take them out to eat. It models for them that everyone needs to grow, everyone needs to be teachable, own their weaknesses, and be willing to be held accountable for their actions. After you complete this section, the parents edit the contract on their computer, print it, and everyone signs it, dates it, and displays it somewhere in a public area of the house. Here is what the contract looks like in full:[20]

---

[20] You can go to https://www.becomingmore.com/resources-and-forms and find a downloadable contract.

FAMILY EXPECTATIONS CONTRACT

Principle #1: To train and equip our children to be independent, autonomous, mature, and effective adults.
Principle #2: It is all about training in impulse control mastering "Duty/discipline before dopamine".
Principle #3: Master consistency in parenting
Principle #4: Create a way for the child to be able to be restored and make it right. If the child receives a consequence that takes away a privilege, then offer a way for them to be restored and get it back by adding a chore (if the privilege is an activity that is occurring soon), or by educating themselves on the core issue by reading a book, doing research, and writing a report.

EXPECTATIONS	CONSEQUENCE/REWARD
KIDS' EXPECTATIONS	
Get A's and B's on all assignments.	Reward: If all "A's" & "B's" on their report card, then (child) will receive $50. Reward: If all "A's" on report card, then (child) gets $200. Consequence: If any grade for an assignment or test or quiz comes in below a "B", then no electronics until the next grade in the class is an "A" or "B".
Daily chores completed immediately after homework completed Weekly chores completed by noon on Saturday (List of chores on back)	Consequence: If chore not completed on time or to standard of parent, the child must immediately complete the chore, and a "deep clean" chore will be added (such as cleaning the toilet, the bathtub, the sink) and must be completed immediately after the first chore. Reward: If child succeeds by being independent and completes all chores without needing to be reminded for one week, then parent will take child to the restaurant of her choice (or a store to buy something $10 limit).

Be respectful (as measured by parents) when asked to complete a task not in list of chores.	**Consequence:** Must immediately obey and will be assigned another task.
Independence and autonomy in tasks.	**Consequence:** If child has the capability and responsibility of doing the task, but asks someone else to do it because of laziness, child must immediately do the task and then serve another member of the family by doing a task for them.
Be at bus stop by 7:00 am	**Consequence:** If bus driver and students need to wait for child, child will write a letter of apology to bus driver and students that is to be read the next school day when child boards the bus.
No swearing (verbally or text)	**Consequence:** Child is to write a letter of apology to recipient of swear word. Letter is to include apology to person for disrespecting them, description of understanding that swearing is inappropriate, immature, and displays a lack of intelligence in word choice, and promise to honor the person and God in the future.
Equip/Empower or Enable?	If the child wants something out of the blue (to do something or buy them something), ask yourself and/or your spouse, "If I/we did this for them or bought this for them, would I/we be a gracious parent, or would I be enabling them?" If enabling, then it is "no". Or if the child misbehaves, ask, "If I/we just verbally corrected them and didn't give them a consequence, would I/we be a gracious parent, or would I be enabling them?" If enable, do "Delay of Sentencing" below.

Delay of Sentencing	If they do something that is inappropriate, disobedient, disrespectful, etc. then mom and dad will simply say, "There will be a consequence for what you did/didn't do" and then will discuss the appropriate consequence together and will communicate the consequence at some indetermined point in the future (no statute of limitations).
1-2-3	If mom/dad asks the child to do something (like pick up the living room), they will be asked, and then if the child delays in doing the task, the next statement will be, "This is #2, if I have to ask again, there will be a consequence". If there is still no response, the task must be done immediately, with another chore added to it, to be done immediately.
	MOM'S EXPECTATIONS
	Consequence:
	DAD'S EXPECTATIONS
	Consequence:

Child 1: _____ *Date:* _____

Child 2: _____ *Date:* _____

Child 3: _____ *Date:* _____

Mom: _____ *Date:* _____

Dad: _____ *Date:* _____

A Few Thoughts on Step-Parenting

About half of the families in our country are blended. On top of the dynamics found within a normal marriage and family context, there are some very unique aspects of the blended family with which I would like to help. Step-parenting can be very difficult because of the difference in bonds between biological and stepparents. Biological parents have three bonds with their children, namely biological, legal, and relational. When the stepparent comes into the picture, the only bond that is possible for the stepparent to develop with their stepchild is relational. It is true that they could develop a legal bond via adoption, but that is only logically possible after the relational bond is created. On top of that, the differences between a stepmom and a stepdad are also very different. Because most children live predominantly with their bio mom, I want to focus on the situation where there is a bio mom, a stepdad, and children of the mom in the home. When the bio-children of the dad stay with the family, it has much more of a "visiting" feeling. Again, it has its unique dynamics, but the principles will apply for all the various types of blended families.

When I work with blended families in the above scenario, the saying, "same story, different day," applies, or better said, "same story, different family." In the dating process, there is a lot of discussion about what the relationship will look like between the stepdad and the stepchildren, with many stating principles such as, "I want to be a great dad" and "I want you to lead my kids." However, they do not take into consideration one key factor: the only bridge he can use to influence his stepchildren is relational,

This technique would be good for every single person on Earth to master and use frequently.

The second technique that we need to master is to *replace giving advice with asking questions*. Think of questions in the categories of past, present, future. You can ask questions about the past, such as the chronology of events that led up to the current situation. On the present, you can ask questions about what your partner is currently feeling and all the implications of the situation. The most important is asking questions about the future. This is where you turn your advice into questions. Instead of saying, "You need to tell your friend . . . !" Instead of this forceful, non-empathic approach, turn it into a question. Ask, "What do you think is best? Are you going to text your friend to lay out the issue clearly or do you think it's better to meet face-to-face?" If you use these two techniques while spoiling them, you will have what you truly want to have: access to their hearts.

have used your positional authority to get your way in the home though, right? I know I'm being hard, but I must be blunt to shake some of you out of the egoistic mindset of proving your worth via your position . . . it never, ever works. If it doesn't work at your job, it won't work at home.

If you signed up to be a big brother, how would you go about having influence in *that* child's life? You would spend a lot of time building relationship and at some point, after a lot of conversation and relationship, they will be open to your counsel. Remember the old adage *they won't care how much you know until they know how much you care*. Delete, eradicate, annihilate all positional power (except setting boundaries on disrespect). When you take your stepchildren anywhere, just you and one of them or all of them, be relaxed and ask them questions about their lives. After a while, small talk turns into deep talk. Use the two techniques I gave earlier to ensure we don't give advice to our spouses but fulfill the role of sounding boards. Here are the two active listening techniques again:

The first technique is the common skill of paraphrasing, or empathy. *Restate, using synonyms, what you heard your child say they are feeling and what the facts are to their story. Restate not only the explicit message (actual words spoken), but also the implicit message (not actually spoken, but definitely a factor impacting the story). Use the format, "You're (emotions), because of (facts, details, story)."* For example, *"You're frustrated because your teacher never seems to compliment you or validate you, but only correct you."* Almost all of us know this technique, but almost all of us are very poor at using it!

out of your stepchildren. Yes, you heard me right. Spontaneously buy things for them, take them out for coffee, to their fast-food places, and to events. Be the fun stepdad. Your measurement of when you have done enough of this is first, your wife confronts you about spoiling them too much (don't stop; that's a good first sign so she can't accuse you of not loving them and being too harsh), and second, when your stepchildren start approaching you wanting to talk about their struggles or to complain about their mom (that's the true win!). You obviously will support your wife, but these are clear signs you are doing it right, and that it's working! Think about it; when you move into the house, you don't have a true "dad" relationship with them. They are nervous and scared to have you in the home, especially when their dad isn't around. Hopefully their bio dad is involved in their life, but even if he isn't, they still have allegiance to him, and that is a *good* thing. It's the way God designed it. Don't think position, think relationship. How do great leaders in companies lead? They are teachable and they are great listeners. What are the worst leaders like? The opposite, plus they use their position to get influence. "Well, I'm the boss, so do it."

There is a saying, "If you have to say you're the leader, you aren't." Why? Because leadership is influence, not position. If you must state your position as the man of the house to gain influence, then you don't have any influence. There is one topic that you can and should use your positional power in the home to make sure certain things happen: spiritual leadership. You absolutely can say, "I am the man of the house, and it is my responsibility to make sure we practice our faith, so we will read the Scriptures, go to church, and serve in ministry." Have you ever said that? But I'm sure you not positional. Most stepdads enter the family thinking positional, such as "I'm the man of the house," expecting stepchildren to automatically honor and like him because of this. When he attempts to set boundaries, correct, or discipline the stepchildren, the positional bridge collapses. The stepchildren complain to their mom about how he made them feel, and the stepmom tries to emphasize his position in the family, but then attempts to rescue them emotionally. He doesn't feel backed up, especially if she pushes back in front of her children, and the bridge comes tumbling down. The stepdad focuses on "what" he is right about, and his wife agrees, but focuses on "how" he went about implementing his goal.

Let's get right to the point. Stepdads, the only power your position has is to set boundaries on your stepchildren actively disrespecting you. Your position means nothing when it comes to the inherent *influence* you want to have in the home. The only bond you have to work with is relational. That's it, so you need to pour into building the foundation of that bridge first. What does that mean? Do not correct or discipline your stepchildren in any way, shape, or form (to begin with). You can set boundaries on the spot if lines are crossed, but you can't implement consequences. If you and your wife use everything in this book, then you can have weekly discussions on parenting just between you and your wife and can come up with a plan of implementation. Include the rule and consequences in the family expectations contract, with your wife acting as the accountability partner and enforcing consequences initially.

This is what I want you to do if you and your wife conclude the relational bridge needs some work: spoil the living daylights